# A BIBLICAL FORMULA FOR FIRE

## ELEMENTS of REVIVAL

## 20

From the author of The Terror of Hell

## JOHN BURTON

20 Elements of Revival

Published by Significant Publishing

ISBN-13: 978-1461088929
ISBN-10: 1461088925

Printed in the United States of America

To my parents, Robert and Barbara Burton.
You poured into me, and continue to do so.
The DNA of a prayer warrior has passed
from one generation to the next.

I will ensure the trend continues.

John Burton is a church planter, conference speaker and author with a mandate to see the fire of God's presence invade cities and nations. He planted Revolution Church in Manitou Springs, Colorado and Revival Church in Detroit, Michigan.

John's ministry style could be described as wildly passionate, engaging, humorous and loaded with the flow and power of the Holy Spirit.

The prevailing theme of the ministry God has given John revolves around the topic of 'being with God'. Where God is, things happen. In His presence, the place where He is, is the fullness of joy. As we discover the wonderful mystery of walking in the Spirit, praying always and making aggressive strides in faith, life becomes incredible!

It truly is an experience in the invisible realm. As we tangibly experience God through deep and active prayer we are interacting 'in the Spirit'. As we walk by faith and understand how amazing a Holy Spirit driven life is, being a believer quickly becomes the greatest adventure on earth!

John is currently focused on teaching, consulting, writing and ministering to churches. If you would like to invite John to speak at your church, conference, camp or other event, please visit www.johnburton.net.

# CONTENTS

# T H E   V I S I O N
## *REVOLUTION*

A s of the last national census in the United States, there are 19,355 recognized cities, or 'incorporated places' in the nation. While there are certainly pockets of heavy Holy Spirit activity, and there is certainly church growth being experienced in many places, as of this writing there are no cities experiencing reportable revival. None.

The contention of this book is simple—*the extreme manifest presence of God is the biblical norm for a New Testament Believer.* We label it many way—revival, an outpouring, renewal—and certainly, different moves of God have distinct flavors to them. However, regardless of the descriptive term we attach to it, we simply are not experiencing it.

What is even more disturbing than this is the fact that there is little sense of urgency to press toward revival. Allow me to make a qualifying statement: many are contending night and day for revival, yet, most are not.

My own city of Manitou Springs, Colorado and our neighbor Colorado Springs are not experiencing 'the river' of revival, and I know I will be held responsible for my handling of that reality. God's dream is for Manitou Springs to be a dwelling place of His presence. The vision is for the entire city to be His. From border to border, Manitou Springs will one day be known as a place of heavy, unusual and perpetual Holy Spirit activity. My job, along with others, is to ensure this dream of my Father comes to pass—and very quickly.

Just as we don't attempt to start driving a car in fifth gear, we should understand that the pursuit of revival must begin at the appropriate place. As we move through the gears, we will find ourselves picking up speed and momentum toward the goal of a city-wide outpouring of the Holy Spirit!

This book will unfold an ancient and emerging structure from the book of Acts that will set us upright on a foundation of fire—the city church.

## THE REVOLUTION HOUSE OF PRAYER STORY

This is not the complete story—that would take thousands of pages. This is the story of birthing, breaking and fire.

In 1991 God spoke very clearly to me as I was in my bathroom in Dayton, Ohio. "John, I've called you to take a city." That simple call has gripped me since, and it continues to grow well beyond my own ability to see it come to pass. It's truly an impossible mission prescribed by a God with whom all things are possible.

In 2001 my wife Amy and I rented a 700 square foot building for me to pray on site in Manitou Springs. Almost immediately people started to wander in and Revolution Church was birthed.

We started as a ministry of prayer. We would prayer-walk the city every week in addition to other weekly prayer events. The vision was becoming vivid and more exciting.

Something subtly happened as the months and years went by, however. While we have always been a ministry of prayer and passion with a heavy emphasis on apostolic advance, worship, the prophetic and other flows of the Holy Spirit, the vision was slowly being compromised.

As more people started to show up, each bringing their own expectations of what a church experience should be, *the demands of ministry started to overwhelm the demands of the vision.*

Now, allow me to make something very clear. The vision never left me. The passion and tears continued to burn and flow. If I would have taken inventory at that stage of the ministry I would have felt pretty good about the pursuit of the prize of city-wide revival.

But, looking back I can now see that the extreme nature of our calling required an extreme pursuit with one hundred percent participation of those who were in partnership with us. Our Sunday services were lively and full of joy and passion. There were some wonderful people enjoying the presence of God each week and I'm blessed to know them to this day. Yet, the mission was not even close to being strategically structured and fulfilled. The expectations of what a 'church' is demanded a certain structural adherence that caused us to violate God's calling for Revolution Church to be a ministry of unified prayer, warfare and fire.

## "YOU'RE DONE."

It is common for me to spend my days in prayer. One day that started as many others had, I was at Revolution Church enjoying God in intercession. I was pacing around the room, laying on my face, declaring the heart of God, resting in His presence and enjoying other facets of my relationship with Jesus. Then, a strange message, delivered directly from the throne of God, arrived in my spirit.

"You're done."

"Excuse me?" I thought. Again, God said, "You're done." Okay. My mind was bothered, but my spirit soaked up this surprising Word of the Lord. I didn't fully understand it, but God was about to reintroduce this ministry to the extreme pursuit of the vision.

The next day at the church I met a lady who was a friend of someone whom I recently met. She looked at me and said, "God says that you are done." I'm sure my face turned white as I started to cry. The anointing in that moment was overwhelming. Two days in a row, God directly revealed his plans.

Over the next few weeks, eight different people, many of whom I had never met, gave me the same prophetic word. I was done. I was also a mess as I wrestled with something that was both irritating to my intellect and powerfully satisfying to my inner-man.

## "DO YOU TRUST ME?"

As I was considering the scope of this fresh word from heaven, I once again was startled by the voice of my Father. I was asleep one night on the couch in my living room. I suddenly awakened and God immediately asked me, "Do you trust me?"

Oh wow! A loaded question from my Dad! Knowing that I was about to venture into a very challenging season of life, I told Him that I did.

What he said next caused my spirit to dance and my mind to wonder.

"You are to transition from ministering to people to ministering to Me."

While I didn't realize it at the moment, I was about to be launched into the most challenging and exciting phase of ministry I had ever experienced. The city of Manitou Springs was being prepared as a city of refuge for the nations. A place of extreme Holy Spirit activity where the voice of God would be heard easily, healings would be continual and intercession would rise night and day from America's mountain, Pikes Peak.

God was taking me from a place of immediate ministry focus to a broader view of the nations. Potentially millions will come to know Jesus through the warfare and breakthrough that happens in Manitou Springs.

As Believers keep the fire on America's mountain burning night and day, and as we are entertaining a powerful flow of the Holy Spirit and extreme angelic activity, demonic networks around the world will be shattered. A massive end-time revival is coming, and God is preparing many portals in geographic regions around the world. These portals of activity will be spiritual mission command centers as revival is planned, launched and administered.

Obviously this mission required something much different than a traditional church! We need Acts Chapter Two to explode again!

What I didn't realize when I received that word on the couch that night was that many others had received similar directives. I visited International House of Prayer (IHOP) in Kansas City shortly after hearing that word, and I was stunned at what I learned. Many others were also transitioning their churches into houses of prayer.

As I found myself at the most significant crossroad in my ministry life, I told the Lord something he already knew. "God, if we challenge the people to launch into this type of ministry, I have a strong feeling that many will leave." And, with a smile on my face I told the Lord, "And our finances just may take quite a hit."

God reminded me of a very powerful vision I had a year or so previous. We had peaked at around 150 people at Revolution Church, and were regularly running around 100. In the vision I saw these 100 people. Suddenly the group shrank to around 35 or so. God told me that he was going to prune—and I didn't like it one bit! After all, we had worked so hard to get programs in place, staff hired and the necessary systems to support those 100 people. We were probably the largest church in this small yet challenging city and I had aspirations of seeing it grow to 200 and well beyond. Then, in the vision, I saw the group of 35 start to glow. It was like they swallowed plutonium! The power was intense! God told me that he would take the city with a group of focused and unified people. God was forming us into a ministry of sold-out, radical, fire-breathing specialists—people who knew God, who prayed hours a day and who owned the vision for Manitou Springs.

Then, back at my crossroads a year later, as I was encouraged by the memory of this vision, it took just a moment to make the transition. Revolution Church was now Revolution House of Prayer.

Since then, the idea of attempting to facilitate every ministry under one roof has dissolved. I started telling people who needed clarification as to who we are that we are the prayer and worship department of the city church. Another way we say it is that we are a prophetic expression of the city church.

What takes place under this roof is but a part of what will happen under the 'roof' of the city church. We were not called to do it all, but rather to help establish a structure on a city level. This structure will result in a cohesive and strategically administered church. Every leader in the city will assume their specialized position on the city church staff. As every leader in the city prays together hours a week, and as we are aligned and positioned correctly, the entire city will be both shaken and taken for the Kingdom.

# INTRODUCTION
## *THE CITY CHURCH*

I was at dinner the other night with a pastor and his wife from another city in Colorado. The issue of the city church came up and I was asked if a monthly networking meeting with other pastors was an important element in the formation of the city church.

The opinion that I shared with them was, "It doesn't work." Is it good? Sure. Is it healthy? It can be. Is it a picture of the city church? No.

I've been involved in such attempts at friendship, unity and support among pastors and other spiritual leaders in a city. I've never seen such meetings result in God's government being established on a city level. Some good can come of such a strategy, but as of yet, revival hasn't arrived.

I'm always intrigued with meeting other pastors, hearing about their ministries and developing new friendships, but I've yet to see a true city church birthed out of such a strategy.

We'll see in the next chapter that the launching of a local church, much less a city church, on the foundation of relationship is the wrong approach. The ancient and emerging structure is one of distinctive apostolic leadership, accountability, a common and specific goal and measurable results.

Again, remember, the challenge of seeing a city church like this is extreme. Revival will be a distinguishing mark of such a church.

The easiest way to envision this is to simply expand the walls of your local church to the north, south, east and west–all the way to the point where the entire city is under that roof.

Now, start asking some questions about your newly envisioned city church:

1. What is God's specific vision for the city church?
2. Who are the apostolic leaders?
3. Who are the pastors, teachers, evangelists, prophets, etc.?
4. What type of reorganization of roles will take place?
5. What will the youth ministry of the city look like?
6. Where will the training department be?
7. Where will the prayer room be?
8. What local church programs and ministries are a threat to the development of the city church?
9. What local church programs and ministries will lend great strength and support to the development of the city church.

The possible questions are endless, but you get the point. The new pastor of the city church may or may not be your pastor. Some pastors may be moved into roles that better fit their gift mix. Some will be mostly counseling while others are mostly teaching while others are mostly evangelizing. The members of the city church won't visit one building every week, but rather will visit the worship center one day, enroll in training on another day, be involved in a small group another day and serve in a soup kitchen another day. And, we'll be in the house of prayer every day!

Of course, that's simply an example, but the point is that one ministry will not have the responsibility of fulfilling every aspect of ministry. Redundancy will be largely eliminated.

The secular world has it figured out–you won't see a Pizza Hut on one corner and another Pizza Hut on the opposite corner. Within a neighborhood, people will frequent many different businesses. They will fill their car with gas in one place, shop for groceries in another, send their children to school in another and buy a book in another. This is an example of God's city church—many different expressions of ministry in many different places within a single neighborhood, all submitted and connected in the governmental structure that's led by humble and anointed apostolic servant leaders.

You may be thinking that such a spiritual experience is simply not possible in today's demanding American lifestyle. *Well, as long as those demands outweigh the demands of Scripture the idea of the city church will die on the drawing board.*

The cares of life will destroy any hopes for city-wide revival. Those who are truly hungry will crave to be with God, together with other people, many times a week. It's all about trusting God's system, enjoying Him, desiring more and being mission-minded!

Now, whether you are embracing the city church or are in a place of developing your local church, the rest of this book will work for you. Local churches are great God-ordained methods of ministry. However, they are not an end in themselves. So, keep in mind the greater picture.

With that, the question is now, "Where do we start in the development, or re-development, of the church?"

Remember, Revolution Church had to morph into Revolution House of Prayer after five years of ministry. You may also have to start fresh, eliminate programs, risk losing the crowds and financial support. Can God be trusted in such a process? Yes.

## THE EMERGING 24/7 CHURCH

As we progress toward the 24/7 church, revival is the vehicle bringing calibration to the biblical model of the church.

I've written books and articles and taught countless messages on the emerging 24/7 church that's coming to this nation. I've been convinced that it would take a revival atmosphere to finally draw people together every night—into the 24/7 model—simply because they would then be convinced that there was literally no better place to be or no more important thing to do than encounter God and advance strategically in mission with others.

## A PROPOSAL: THE FLEX CHURCH STRUCTURE

Local churches have the unique position of either being a great threat to a regional outpouring, or a great strength. The demands of the regional, corporate gathering are increasing in intensity, and any competing activity (within the church or outside of it) will put the greater city mission at risk. In order for the purpose of this book to be realized, we have to put the Isaacs of our own local ministry focuses and agendas on the altar. The local must give way to the regional. The regional mission must have priority over the local mission.

Here's an example of what I'm trying to communicate: I was asked to be the keynote speaker at The Palace (where the Detroit Pistons play) where an all-city church outreach was planned. Sadly, churches refused to cancel their own local Wednesday night services so their people could support the event. So, the regionally focused event was cancelled. Do you see what I mean? City impact was forfeited for the sake of lesser, local activities.

Here's the *Flex Church Structure* proposal: Local churches will have a primary local church service that trumps most everything else. They might meet on Sunday mornings, for example, and have a high bar of expectancy that their local congregation will gather together. Additionally, they would have vision-driven, prayer-fueled local church meetings at other times of the week (Bible studies, youth meetings, small groups, etc.). However, they must be ready to flex—to give way to the demands of the greater regional focus. If a regional call is sounded, pastors will then cancel the local ministry (with the possible exception of their main, Sunday morning service) and lead their congregations to that event.

Additionally, we as leaders must have open hands and release the people under our care into other churches and ministries. The regular schedule may include Sunday morning at your church, Sunday evening at a house of prayer, Monday evening at a church well known for its strengths in teaching, Tuesday evening in a Bible study at another ministry, etc. throughout the rest of the week.

The 24/7 church will:

1. Be regionally focused
2. Include participation with multiple ministries and churches each week

So, if there's a Bible study on a Tuesday night, but a spontaneous, God initiated fire is lit in another part of the city, then cancel the

Bible study and lead the people to the fire. If there's a youth meeting on a Friday night, cancel that and head to the regional event that God is uniquely moving in. But, by all means, lets keep the city church open and active continually!

In the midst of a three-week outpouring in Detroit, one pastor cancelled everything in his local church, *including Sunday mornings*, and led his congregation to the fire every single night of the week! What leadership this is! A Kingdom mindset like this is what I am talking about!

## WHAT IF SOMEONE NEEDS GOD ON A MONDAY NIGHT?

Check out what Pastor Joe Sazyc wrote in the midst of a 21-day outpouring in Dearborn Heights, Michigan:

*Something hit me last night after the service... I could do this til Jesus comes! Yes, I the guy who didn't want nightly meetings in the beginning!*

*There is a hunger in this city! Word is spreading.*

*What if someone needs God on a Monday night? Do they need to wait for Sunday to have a touch of glory? And what if the glory doesn't "fall" that Sunday or NEVER falls in their church? I am being haunted by Brian Simmons' phrase a while back... "God doesn't just want you to have a house of prayer here, he wants you to have a house of GLORY!" All this is reminding me of a passion I have had for years, but all my busyness has stifled in recent months. I have always believed church should be 24/7! Even long before I knew about 24/7 prayer and before IHOP or anything like that existed! I've got to believe a major metro area like Detroit (especially one being marked by God for Awakening) can certainly sustain at least nightly meetings if not 24/7.*

*All that to say, I'm so hungry for this, I'm tempted to keep this thing going after the 21 days, even if no one were to go with me. It may not look exactly like what we have now, but SOMETHING that invites God's GLORY needs to continue nightly. The Fireplace cannot go out! I KNOW I cannot do it on my own, so I pray our team stays intact and even grows. I pray we begin to see an influx of crazy people who will staff this thing as musicians, ushers, tech people, etc… I think we need to AGGRESSIVELY pray for laborers (Matt. 9) and resources. What's encouraging is that I believe GOD wants this. We won't be bending a reluctant arm!*

Notice Joe's call for laborers. This is a primary reason why the local churches must give way to the regional focus. The people in your churches are needed to work elsewhere in the region!

Additionally, they need to be infused with the fire, and will have an opportunity to learn how to work in such a way that their fruit is felt well beyond the walls of the local church.

Yes, a reformation in the church is an absolute must. It will take great humility to admit that the outpouring in a region most probably will not initiate in your local church. With that being the case, we must keep our radars on and look for the place where the fire is lit–and move out to that place and offer to serve with expediency.

# E L E M E N T   O N E

## *AGREEMENT*

---

*Acts 2:1 When the Day of Pentecost had fully come, they were all with one accord in one place.*

The way this ancient and emerging church was birthed is the way it was meant to continue. God drew zealots together to actively wait.

As we step through these twenty elements, it's critical to prayerfully consider the step-by-step process. It is flexible enough to allow God to infuse your local church growth experience with your own DNA, yet the underlying principles simply must not be violated.

This first element is the most critical, yet is probably the most neglected. In the pursuit of establishing a new local church, or in the development of an existing one, the pure adrenaline of it can cause us to become impatient. We need to understand the first church in the book of Acts could not have been planted from a human perspective.

Good teaching, proven programs, intimate small groups, evangelistic crusades and other methods would not work at this stage of the process. These are actually parts of future elements that will take root and develop further in the church planting process.

So, what is this first element?

The verse tells us that they were ALL in one accord AND in one place. This depicts a mature and hungry team of radically devoted Believers who understand the massive commitment it will take to fulfill the mission.

To launch, there must be a strategic team of mission-minded owners of the vision.

A tragic mistake that is often made at this initial phase of ministry is the improper focus on relationship. Fellowship will become a staple of the church experience well into the process, but to entrust the strategy of fellowship as a foundational element at this phase will result in failure, stagnation and a lack of power.

Being in agreement is very different than being in fellowship. An attitude of agreement results in corporate strength that will bust through many barriers the enemy will set up in the early stages.

A strategy of fellowship alone is incredibly susceptible to offenses taking root, gossip, frustration, disagreement and the fostering of an Absalom spirit. Fellowship is simply not strong enough to be a foundation of a local church. Agreement, however, easily is.

Consider the Acts 1:8 mandate:

*Acts 1:8 But you shall receive power when the Holy Spirit has come upon you; and you shall be witnesses to Me in Jerusalem, and in all Judea and Samaria, and to the end of the earth.*

The mandate was to gather together and wait for power for a specific purpose. Of course, we know that the call is to be witnesses, but do we understand what that means? It's not to simply pass out tracts at the mall. The greek meaning of the word witnesses in this passage is *mar'-toos*. Martyrs. We are called to embrace the call to die for Christ.

If we gather people with the purpose of fellowship and nurturing as the primary focus, people will tend to respond based on what they receive from the church. But, on the contrary, when the gathered people understand the severity of the mission, that their mandate is to embrace the call to martyrdom, they aren't looking for personal gain at all. They are surrendered to the call to advance the Kingdom in the city in deliberate unity.

I'll often hear pastors state that they are launching a new church on a foundation of fellowship. They have a plan of worshiping together, inviting friends and developing a new community. Of course, the heart behind this is wonderful. Strategically however it simply rarely works.

This first element of agreement breeds the second element that we'll discuss further in a moment. The second element is extreme devotion of time. We'll notice that the first church was together every day. Why? Because that was how it was birthed. In order to capture God's heart, hear His instructions, nurture unity and become alert to the directives of apostolic leadership we must be together nearly continually.

If we are fellowship minded, this type of commitment will rarely last. Desire for fellowship is inward focused primarily, but an attitude of agreement causes us to look outward. To be agreed and unified toward an impossible goal that God has presented to the team will both require and result in a continual pursuit of that goal together.

I often teach that if we are to experience revival, we must do now what we will be doing when revival breaks out. A revival atmosphere results in people craving to be in the church building night after night to be further empowered. Prayer and worship and breaking under the presence of God never end. If we are contending for that, we must start the process now.

I find it amazing that churches are eliminating services in response to a very demanding American lifestyle. If we are to experience revival, we must fight that spirit and once again, as in the previous generation, be in the church every time the doors are open—and the doors should be open night and day!

## THE EXPERIENCE

At the risk of getting ahead of myself, I want to share now what we are contending for. The biblical norm for Believers is to experience the weighty presence of the Holy Spirit regularly. The normal experience for a Sunday service, for example, is for us to walk in the door and immediately become influenced by an atmosphere of fire. Brokenness, tears, drunkenness in the Holy Spirit, prophetic unction, repentance and other manifestations should be the expected reality day after day. It's truly a 2 Chronicles 7 church that we need!

> *2 Chronicles 7:1-3 When Solomon had finished praying, fire came down from heaven and consumed the burnt offering and the sacrifices; and the glory of the LORD filled the temple. And the priests could*

*not enter the house of the LORD, because the glory of the LORD had filled the LORD'S house. When all the children of Israel saw how the fire came down, and the glory of the LORD on the temple, they bowed their faces to the ground on the pavement, and worshiped and praised the LORD, saying: "For He is good, For His mercy endures forever."*

The glory was so extreme that everybody hit the pavement outside and worshiped! When we experience power like that, and like in Acts chapter two, the ability to advance the Kingdom, win souls and experience miracles increases significantly.

We have become satisfied with teaching services, song services, social gatherings and other activities without the baptism of fire that should be burning through them.

I often discuss what I call the *money changer principle*. Churches, both new and mature, often have an imbalanced focus on satisfying the needs and desires of the members. Church growth strategies dictate that we must have certain things in place if we expect people to want to come to our church. So, from the outset, our minds are tilted toward drawing the crowds, and in order to do that we ask the question, *"What will cause people to come, stay and get involved?"*

May I offer that this mindset must change if we are to experience God the way He wants to be experienced. The money changers' table was overturned by Jesus. He was indignant. He stated clearly that the temple was to be a house of prayer. What was the sin of the money changers? *They went into the temple with the expectation of leaving with more than they entered with.* The temple is to be a place of sacrifice! We are to have the expectation of leaving with less than we entered with!

My favorite definition of the word religion is:

*Man's attempt to use God to get what he wants*

The money changes used God and used God's structure of the church for personal gain. This must stop.

If we as leaders understand this, we will have no problem requiring much from those who are joined with us in mission. We are truly called to die, to agree with the call to martyrdom. That perspective must be embraced and shouted from the rooftops.

Let's look at an interesting passage of scripture. Keep in mind as you read this that Peter was the *rock* on which the church was birthed. Jesus was making a severe statement not only to Peter but also to the soon to be developed church.

> *Matthew 16:21-25 From that time Jesus began to show to His disciples that He must go to Jerusalem, and suffer many things from the elders and chief priests and scribes, and be killed, and be raised the third day. Then Peter took Him aside and began to rebuke Him, saying, "Far be it from You, Lord; this shall not happen to You!" But He turned and said to Peter, "Get behind Me, Satan! You are an offense to Me, for you are not mindful of the things of God, but the things of men." Then Jesus said to His disciples, "If anyone desires to come after Me, let him deny himself, and take up his cross, and follow Me. For whoever desires to save his life will lose it, but whoever loses his life for My sake will find it."*

Note a very important statement that Jesus made:

*"You are an offense to Me, for you are not mindful of the things of God, but the things of men."*

Peter unwittingly renounced the cross. Jesus rebuked him in this famous conflict to ensure that the generations to come would be sure to embrace what Peter renounced—daily death under the weight of a cross.

This was exceedingly critical not only for Peter and not only for the generations, but primarily for the structure that Peter represented—the church. We don't renounce the call to death, and we don't use the church, as the money changers did, for personal gain. We gather in radical agreement and we lay down our own agendas and desires for the sake of the mission.

As we launch or redevelop our churches according to this New Testament paradigm we must be sure that we avoid a structure that appeals to man ahead of God. Jesus told Peter that he was an offense to Him. Why was he an offense? After all, he wanted Jesus to be safe and comforted. The boldness of Peter that we saw in the garden as Jesus was being led away to his destiny with the cross showed itself in this instance as well.

We don't know what other inner struggles Peter may have been dealing with, but we do know that Jesus didn't appreciate his reaction to those struggles. He stated clearly that to be mindful of man ahead of God was offensive.

Our churches must be setup primarily to minister to God on a foundation of prayer, sacrifice, offerings and service. When someone comes into our church as a visitor they should witness a radical atmosphere of extreme commitment, passion and mission-driven fervor. Instead of forming materials that emphasize what the visitor can expect from their new church those materials should highlight what their new church expects from them!

Churches are missional organizations. They exist to accomplish a mission—and to equip the saints to ensure that mission advances with precision. We must be mindful of God and the vision he has given that church.

## VISION?

I won't go into much detail here, but I believe the concept of vision must be addressed at least to a point. Agreement will not last without a vivid and easily communicated vision.

I was leading a prayer event at a church in the area on a Friday night earlier this year. One of the other leaders who was with me that night asked the pastor what his vision was. When it was obvious the pastor was struggling with this question we asked if he had anything written down so we could read it and then come into agreement with them during our prayer time. He went searching for something to give us, and finally found a brochure that described the church's mission.

Vision for our mission should consume us night and day. If we do not lead from a place of vision, we will go nowhere. If we don't have vision, we need to ask some hard questions. Are we the one to lead the church? What alternate role may God be opening up to us?

The process of gaining vision might include something as simple as praying and fasting on a mountain somewhere for a few days. God desires every one of us to have clear vision—but to receive that vision takes an absolute dedication to being with God, hearing His voice and obeying. Yes, our dreams and desires may be threatened when God starts talking, but as we walk in the direction of God's voice, we will shake nations!

Simply, if we don't have vision, we may need to step down. However, if we do have vision, stepping down won't even be an option. There is a job to be done!

A trap that many men and women of God fall into is assuming a leadership role based on gifting instead of vision and calling. Someone who has a pastoral gifting may not be called to lead a church at all. A teacher may be called as a small group leader or a lecturer or an author. Or, that person may indeed be called to lead a church, but if that is the case, vision must burn like a fire in their bones!

I'll finish this sub-point by saying this–vision is very specific and personal. Vision is not a quote we hang on the wall in our sanctuary like, "Our mission is to grow closer to God and each other." Vision is precise and seemingly impossible to fulfill. It will cause great excitement and scrutiny to be aroused at the same time. It will usually include geographical information, statistical goals, clear transformational ideas and a laser focus to fulfill that mission. This doesn't mean it won't be ambiguous at times–the larger the vision, the more difficult it may be to put fully into words. However, there is an end goal and everybody under our leadership will be willing to pay its great price–and they will celebrate when we arrive together.

So, we discovered a lot in this first verse of Acts chapter two. Everybody had a clear vision, was perfectly agreed and together continually. The cost was understood at the very beginning–what was coming required strict adherence to God's structural plan by everybody involved.

## EVALUATION

» **Church planters**–if your team is radically agreed to pursue the fulfillment of a vivid vision for their region, then by all means, keep reading! If there are some in your midst who are wondering what is in it for them, then remain in this phase until you have 100% participation.

» **Existing church leaders**–Your evaluation may be a bit more difficult, especially if you are significantly developed. First of all, don't be afraid to violate existing structures in the fear of losing people. A great reformation is coming to the earth that will cause church as we know it to be shaken to its core. Do you have an atmosphere of extreme agreement and passion for a clear and precise vision? Is there great expectancy of what is to come and great commitment to the realization of that dream? If so, let's move on!

» **Everybody else**–Are you involved with your current church for the right reasons? Would your pastor be able to say that you are one of his most loyal and faithful partners in ministry? Do you embrace the vision to the point of extreme participation and lifestyle change?

# E L E M E N T   T W O
### *AN EXTREME DEVOTION OF TIME*

*Acts 2:1 When the Day of Pentecost had fully come, they were all with one accord in one place.*

Yes, we're still in the first verse! The first element dealt with the first fourteen words of the chapter. This one deals with the next three, "in one place".

When the city church is realized, and when revival breaks out from that structure, we'll see the cares of life finally take a back seat to the cares of the Kingdom. Instead of eliminating corporate gathering times, we'll see the church become a 24-hour entity.

For the truly hungry, there are few excuses that will be strong enough to keep them out of the temple! So, since we must model now what will eventually be the normal experience for Believers in our nation, we must be together—a lot.

The greater the vision, the more important our frequency in gathering becomes. Simply, there is much to be done.

Here at Revolution House of Prayer, I am looking at one of the large white boards on the wall. On it is a crude drawing of an example of what the city church of Manitou Springs will look like. It is in the form of a map of this city with certain significant roads and properties marked. The various properties represent the various departments of the city church. I believe it's a literal depiction of what the church of Manitou Springs will eventually look like–many properties now used for secular purposes will be used for the advancement of the city church.

The most important department for any church, local or city, is the prayer room. Many will attempt to launch a ministry with evangelism, teaching, fellowship or other focuses that were never meant to initiate this far up on the timeline. The first department must be the upper room, the place of contending, prayer, warfare and fire.

Until the house of prayer is developed, there is little sense in launching additional departments. The necessary power, vision and supernatural impartation will not be there. Additionally, it's very important to understand that this department of prayer is not only a foundation for every other ministry, but it is the most significant ministry in and of itself. This cannot be overstated.

On the map there are also many other properties identified. There is a youth building in the middle town, a training center in one of the other church buildings, many pastor led, small group gathering places right downtown, hotels for intern housing, properties for retreats and outreach and other places that will house departments of the city church.

Each department will be led by a person who is gifted to do so. Weekly strategy sessions and lengthy prayer meetings among the teachers, pastors, apostles, prophets, evangelists and other departmental heads will ensure a smoothly operating city church.

Now, let's discuss what an normal individual's weekly experience might look like as they participate in the city church. Remember, we're on element number two which is an emphasis on an *extreme devotion of time.*

## THE SMITH FAMILY'S DAILY SCHEDULE

*John Smith, married to Lucy Smith, father to Sally (1 year old) Mike (13 years old) and Holly (17 years old)*

| Sunday | |
|---|---|
| 8am: | At the house of prayer interceding for the upcoming service |
| 10am: | Worshiping together in their primary weekly church service |
| 6pm: | In a class in the training center across town |
| **Monday** | |
| 12pm: | Lucy and the kids attend noon prayer together |
| 7pm: | After eating dinner together, the Smiths all go to the outreach center next to the park to feed the homeless |
| **Tuesday** | |
| 6pm: | John fasts today, so he skips dinner after work and joins Lucy and the kids to pray in the house of prayer until 9pm |
| **Wednesday** | |
| 12pm: | Lucy and the kids attend noon prayer together |
| 7pm: | John, Lucy and Sally attend a small group in a coffee shop while the older kids are in the youth building for a worship event |
| **Thursday** | |
| 7pm: | The entire family serves in a revival service at the house of prayer |
| **Friday** | |
| 7pm: | At the retreat center for a twelve hour shift of intercession |
| **Saturday** | |
| All Day | John and his family rest and enjoy each other's company |

Of course, this is simply an example, but it is a picture of what happened in the first church in Acts and what we'll see in the years to come. Daily prayer and ministry was the norm. This being the case, it's important that the church is birthed with those who embrace the element of an extreme devotion of time. Raise the bar high now in preparation of a very demanding and thrilling revival experience later.

If we intentionally order our days the excuses will fade away. We'll have more than enough time every week for hours of prayer, ministry, training, service, family time, entertainment and other endeavours.

Often, the cares of life have so gripped people that they will pull out every excuse they can find to avoid submitting to the call of the devotion of extreme time. If we are honest, we would admit that we could easily pull out our daily agenda and find two hours a day to pray. We simply get up earlier, or go to bed later. Even better, we don't show up for the latest movie, stretch out on the couch in front of the TV or involve ourselves in other lesser activities. To give one tenth of our time every day in intentional prayer is easily doable.

Allow me to once again emphasize the purpose of the church. It is not to primarily meet the needs of people, but rather to accomplish a God given mission. It's birthed not on fellowship, but on agreement. Agreement on what? On an extreme vision that will cost much. If someone comes to our church and wonders what they can get out of it they will only go as far, or sometimes just a little further, than they feel they need or want. They will stop when full.

We must not stop when full, we must start when full! We can stop when every person in the city lives in the presence of God, every mission is complete and every dream of God is fulfilled!

When I first started Revolution Church I would often jump through hoops to make sure visitors knew just how much they would love this church. I'd even at times ask them what they wanted and I'd do everything I could to meet that demand. My heart was good, but I was falling into a trap. I was misunderstanding the purpose of the church, and was operating in the same spirit that Peter was when Jesus rebuked him. I was more mindful of man than God. I needed to realize that what God required was much different than what I was presenting.

Now, when people inquire of our ministry I let them know up front that it will cost them a lot. We pray literally 10-30 hours a week or more on site. We believe in extravagant giving of tithes and offerings. It's important to be together several times a week so we can receive fresh instruction, prophetic insight, revelation and understanding of what we are to do. The atmosphere is challenging and thrilling.

So, just who stays after hearing such an invitation to this ministry? Only those who are called here, ready to work and are burning with radical passion. It's only the people who are agreed (element one) and devoted to participate to an extreme degree (element two).

Sure, some do pop in and out and have a lesser degree of participation. That's okay, and I do enjoy seeing these people and I pray they will be gripped by the challenge here, however I know that the mission will be apostolically led by those with a forerunner anointing—those who are bleeding and sweating and bathed in tears for this ministry. The energy and resources that we expend on equipping the saints must be focused on those who will step into their new equipment and run the race with fiery passion. It's how the first church was birthed.

> *Ephesians 4:11-16 And He Himself gave some to be apostles, some prophets, some evangelists, and some pastors and teachers, for the equipping of the saints for the work of ministry, for the edifying of the body of Christ, till we all come to the unity of the faith and of the knowledge of the Son of God, to a perfect man, to the measure of the stature of the fullness of Christ; that we should no longer be children, tossed to and fro and carried about with every wind of doctrine, by the trickery of men, in the cunning craftiness of deceitful plotting, but, speaking the truth in love, may grow up in all things into Him who is the head--Christ-- from whom the whole body, joined and knit together by what every joint supplies, according to the effective working by which every part does its share, causes growth of the body for the edifying of itself in love.*

The goal is to equip with the expectation of people stepping into position to do the work of the ministry. As people are edified in this way, they will find themselves spending a great deal of time serving the ministry and fulfilling their calling.

To train with no expectation of return for the effort is a waste of God's time and resources.

## EVALUATION

Many potential revivals are compromised at this point. Would you say that you and your family are ready to meet the challenge of being in the temple daily? Is the church structured in such a way that results in extreme participation? Are you on the way to being a 100% church—100% of the people participating in an extravagant way? How would you and the others in the church respond if the pastor called for everybody to fast and pray on site for 72 hours? If you've busted through those obstacles, certainly move on to the next element!

# ELEMENT THREE
## *AN EXTREME SPIRIT-FILLED ENVIRONMENT*

---

*Acts 2:2-3 And suddenly there came a sound from heaven, as of a rushing mighty wind, and it filled the whole house where they were sitting. Then there appeared to them divided tongues, as of fire, and one sat upon each of them.*

Churches can't be birthed out of human strength, wisdom or knowledge. It simply must be a supernatural move of the Holy Spirit. In fact, I believe it's mandatory to avoid moving to latter elements until element three and four have become a standard and identifying trait of our ministry. We'll look at element four in a moment.

When I was a youth pastor in the San Diego area I was presented with a request. Every Friday night we would start the night with an hour of passionate prayer and then continue into a night of extreme Spirit-filled worship, preaching and ministry time. We'd start at 6pm and wouldn't end many nights until after 11pm. We made no apologies for our radical behavior. When the weather allowed (which was often in San Diego!) we would set up on the lighted basketball court which was right next to a busy highway. Cars would often honk as they witnessed a bizarre scene of wild dance, lifted hands and seeming disorderly conduct!

One night a core member of the youth group approached me. He wanted to bring his friends, who were not saved, but was convinced they would 'freak out' if they walked into such an environment. He thought a more sedate service would make it easier for them to comfortably encounter Jesus. His intentions were loving and very good, but he had a common mis-understanding of biblical protocol.

Such a mindset is draining the church of its power! I challenged this young man. "Nick, bring them. Bring them and watch what happens."

He did bring them, and they all got saved in the furnace of Holy Spirit activity.

Somewhere along the line many have bought into the idea that a more social and toned down introduction to God would result in mass salva-tions. We forget that without the fire of the Holy Spirit there is little to draw people into a passionate relationship with Jesus!

We don't need another socially tepid atmosphere—we need to invite the Holy Spirit to move among us! We must repent for embracing the idea that we have what it takes to compel people to 'get saved', when in fact it is the supernatural and stunning invasion of an invisible Force into a desperate heart that results in a deep and intimate relationship with our Father!

May there be an expectation of angelic visitations, prophetic activity, signs and wonders, miracles and a fire so hot that anybody that walks into the room falls on their face and cries, "Holy!"

There have been many times in my ministry where God was drawing us into a deeper place corporately. We might be compelled to sit in hushed silence for an extended period of time during a Sunday service, or, quite the opposite, may feel God so strongly that we groan and collapse to the ground.

I'll admit that as I look around at the crowd, and notice that several people are uncomfortable and disconnected, that the temptation is there to tone it down. After all, it wouldn't feel good at all if God moved this week and half the people didn't return next week.

Listen closely—I believe that such an attitude in the coming years will result in a severe judgement from God. We must NOT touch the presence of God lightly. God simply must conduct every corporate meeting. One should rarely look like another. Prophecy, dance, 'groans that cannot be uttered', brokenness, deliverance and other manifestations of the Holy Spirit must be expected, embraced and contended for.

As we do this, many people won't want to come to our churches. Some will. Remember, we are not there to set up a system that will please people, but rather, we have been entrusted with the fearful assignment to develop a temple that will be a dwelling place of the mighty Creator of the universe! Everything we do should be about the presence of God.

As we do this, the unsaved will suddenly find themselves healed, delivered, free from addiction, seeing visions, having dreams, experiencing angels and desperately in love with Jesus!

I made a serious commitment to God and to the current RHOP team. *I would never allow our atmosphere in our prayer events or services to be toned down out of respect of those less hungry.* If a visitor comes through the door, the fire must burn hotter not cooler! Many churches purposely have a less offensive service as their main service and then have a *Believer's service* at another time of the week. How can this be? The purpose of the church IS NOT to draw visitors! It's to be a place of fire and prayer, teaching and challenge.

This element is non-negotiable. A seeker-sensitive program may have its place somewhere within the structure of a church—but not here! Not at this critical stage of the development of a city-wide dwelling place of the Most Holy One!

We must remember the purpose of a church—it is to be a house of prayer for all nations. That is the reason for its existence! If we press in and pray and worship and cry out night and day for weeks, months and years to come, we will experience a perpetual stirring in an atmosphere of fire. Prayer is a primary ministry, not something that simply paves the way for another more important activity. This desperate hunger for God's presence will cause us to dwell with Him for hours on end, day after day. We won't be so worried about a messy church service. We'll err on the side of freedom as people discover how to live a Holy Spirit driven life.

## EVALUATION

Are your corporate services burning hot? Are you experiencing signs, wonders, prophecy, dreams, visions and other moves of God? Is there an extreme dedication to this for the life of your ministry? This house of prayer must burn hot, night and day, forever. This phase of church planting may last months or years. If you are redeveloping an existing church, are you ready to challenge people to depart their current assignments and programs as you corporately pray and contend for fire several nights a week? If your primary purpose is to minister to God, stir a prophetic and anointed atmosphere and always err on the side of freedom, then let's raise the bar and move to the next element.

# ELEMENT FOUR
## *EVERYBODY FILLED WITH THE HOLY SPIRIT*

*Acts 2:4 And they were all filled with the Holy Spirit and began to speak with other tongues, as the Spirit gave them utterance.*

Before the first church went public, everybody in the ministry was filled with the Holy Spirit and spoke with other tongues. A proper handling of element number three (an extreme Holy Spirit filled environment) will simply result in everybody being filled. It's a desperately critical gift that everybody in the church must receive. Power from on high must infuse everybody because the call is too difficult (actually it's impossible) for them to accomplish without it.

While speaking in tongues is wonderful and important, the primary purpose for the in filling of the Holy Spirit is to impart boldness and power into each of us. We won't have the option to simply go to church on a Sunday and call it a day. Each of us will have a severe responsibility to advance the Kingdom of God in a significant way. To do so requires much power and much boldness.

The world in which we're called will resist such an advance of God's

Kingdom. The battles will be fierce. To win, each person needs great supernatural impartation.

Now, I want to prepare you. Whether you are involved in a new church or an established one, the process you must embrace to ensure the fulfillment of this element may actually cause your ministry to settle here for quite some time. The temptation to minimize praying to focus more on evangelism, setting up programs and pursuing church growth must be tempered with what the Holy Spirit will be identifying to you during this very important phase.

Let me explain. The Word tells us that the Holy Spirit is our teacher. As everybody in the camp is agreed, spending a great deal of time together in deep prayer and as all are filled with the amazing gift of the Holy Spirit, God will have great freedom to impart His blueprints.

At Revolution, we have whiteboards on every wall. We are continually hearing God's instructions for our next step. We draw prophetic pictures, words, scriptures and other insights on the boards as God plants them in our spirits. We add to them confirmations and other connecting pieces that add up to an amazing big picture.

The prophetic atmosphere gives us the ability to know what God would have us do, and the boldness and power we receive in this phase gives us the ability to obey.

I recently asked a pastor a question. It came after we had an extreme encounter with a principality of our city on a prayer journey. We had amazing prophetic insight on how to fight the enemy, and then struck with great power.

The question I asked him was, "How do pastors and leaders accomplish their missions if they aren't able to hear God, see in the Spirit and fight the invisible enemy that stands in their way?"

His answer? "They don't."

However, if we are full of the Holy Spirit we will all be able to discern the amazing world of the invisible realm, fight the prevailing demonic spirits in our cities, grow in great faith, flow in great grace and be ready for an effective launching of a city church. Until we discern, fight, grow and flow our city is not ready and neither are we. The development of this element may literally take years.

> *1 Corinthians 14:39 Therefore, brethren, desire earnestly to prophesy,*
> *and do not forbid to speak with tongues.*

*1 Corinthians 14:1 Pursue love, and desire spiritual gifts, but especially that you may prophesy.*

I explain to everybody at RHOP that they must discover their prophetic gifting. Desire that earnestly. As we hear God and proclaim his Word and heed his unique situational instructions we will be in quite a productive position.

## EVALUATION

Is everybody filled in the Holy Spirit? Are they prophesying, dreaming dreams and seeing visions? What strategies of warfare have been revealed? Are your journals or whiteboards filling up with prophetic instruction? Who is going to carry out the various parts of that instruction? What is the principality over your city? How are you going to take it out? If you don't have the answers to these questions, don't move on. You can possibly eliminate marketing and most programs in your church. A broad focus must be replaced with a narrow focus. Settle in for quite a journey–this may take a while.

# E L E M E N T   F I V E

## *INTERNATIONAL RESPONSIBILITY*

*Acts 2:5 And there were dwelling in Jerusalem Jews, devout men, from every nation under heaven.*

As we emerge from the previous element into this one, we should at least partially understanding our responsibility in a great end-time revival.

The obvious conclusion here would be to send missionaries, pray for the nations and be alerted to global events. These focuses are certainly important, but to limit our understanding to them will result in only a partially fulfilled mission.

The successful facilitation of our local and city ministries will result in an exponentially immeasurable advance of ministry around the world—and it goes well beyond supporting missionaries and their families.

Allow me to share a couple of examples with you:

When I first planted Revolution in 2001 I had a vision. This vision would be critical as I was gaining understanding of how Manitou Springs would be connected to the nations of the world. In the vision I was looking at the Earth from outer space. There were many cities that I saw highlighted by a point of light. These cities, the Lord revealed to me, were significant demonic strongholds. There were many, though they were not countless, around the globe. Manitou Springs was one of the cities. The Lord then revealed something very interesting to me. The cities were connected by arcs of light, much like you would see on a map in the front of the magazine that airlines provide in the pocket of the seat back in front of you. The map shows the routes between cities that their airline services.

It was interesting to see how incredibly strategic the enemy is in his global scheme to destroy mankind. I'm certain that in these cities demons of various rankings receive precise and complex instructions from their superiors. It's very much a war room setting in strategic cities around the world.

Then, as I was watching this unfold in front of me, I saw the point of light in Manitou Springs disappear. It represented a successfully completed assignment of spiritual warfare in the city. The principality had been taken out and the communication was disrupted. What I saw next revealed to me our international influence–the arc of light that connected Manitou Springs to other cities and nations also disappeared. Other city's demonic strategies were radically disrupted because of our local success.

As time went on, the Lord revealed to me that Manitou Springs was a demonic headquarters for the nations, and that our primary role in the early stages was to shut down that operation. God desires this city to be transformed into an angelic headquarters for revival in the nations! Literally, international revival would be at least partially conducted from this city! Now that's an international responsibility not to be taken lightly!

Recently I met someone who stated that they felt Manitou Springs was a demonic Norad for the nations! Then, a week later, I received a phone call from an author who said he felt compelled to connect with me. He said that he was writing a book, and was impressed that Manitou Springs was a possible setting for it. He said he saw Manitou Springs as a demonic Norad! Amazing confirmation!

There have been many equally confirming prophetic words and insights that have affirmed this time and again. This is why it is so important to have visions, hear prophetically and understand our unique role in the larger picture. To launch out without an understanding of our international responsibility, without being full of power and boldness and without perfect agreement is simply presumptuous at best and fatal for our ministries and those whom we're to partner with at worst.

The focus on prayer and the prophetic at this stage is very important. We can often find ourselves so zealous to move out into 'real ministry' at the expense of truly making a difference. For example, I have sadly met people who decided against developing a life of prayer as a primary ministry in favor of other ministry pursuits. They were so ready to operate in their gifts of evangelism, teaching, pastoring or other focuses but didn't have the patience or understanding of the importance and effectiveness of a lifestyle of prayer.

I'll often hear people argue against 'just staying in the church and praying all day'. To say such a thing reveals a lack of understanding of the effectiveness and power of prayer as a primary ministry. To be presented with an international responsibility simply demands that we discover the power of lengthy, persistent prayer. We need people who pray hours a day to stay right where they are!

*Isaiah 56:7 Even them I will bring to My holy mountain, And make them joyful in My house of prayer. Their burnt offerings and their sacrifices Will be accepted on My altar; For My house shall be called a house of prayer for all nations.*

Keep in mind—the reason the church exists is to be a house of prayer— for all nations!

I sometimes challenge the wonderfully zealous evangelist (who may not understand his own need to learn to pray hours a day) to take a gospel tract and deliver it to Osama Bin Laden. Witness to him. Lead him to the Lord. Well, of course, this is simply not possible since we don't know where he is. Well, let's adjust the challenge. Witness to the presidents and leaders in the 10/40 Window. What about the teachers in our public schools? We could go on and on. The mission suddenly seems quite impossible.

To have an international focus without understanding the power of lengthy prayer will cause the mission to die. Frustration and discouragement will set in. But, to grasp prayer as the most powerful force in the universe will cause us to rise again with great faith!

We can literally change the entire atmosphere of the cave or home where Osama Bin Laden is hiding—right now! The prophetic fire out of our mouths can do more in a moment than any other missional effort. Add lengthy prayer to evangelism, teaching and other ministry efforts and the fire of revival will reach every people group on earth!

Every person who desires to lead any form of ministry at Revolution House of Prayer must participate in hours of scheduled prayer each week. There is no exception. It's out of the furnace of prayer that cities and nations will be invaded with the life of Jesus Christ.

So, here's the idea–through extreme discipline in prayer, God is going to deliver to us some very unique and challenging directives. These directives will often defy logic, be humanly impossible, unique and special to your mission and region and the proper response to them will result in revival coming more easily in other parts of the world.

## EVALUATION

Have you received insight on your international responsibility? What part do you play? What is unique about that part? Have you journaled dreams and visions and prophetic insights? What type of world vision possesses you and those with you? Would you be able to write down at least a broad step-by-step process for a successful mission? If so, and if you are still burning white hot, continue on to element six.

# ELEMENT SIX
## *IT WILL BE MESSY, DIFFERENT THAN THE CULTURAL NORM*

*Acts 2:6 And when this sound occurred, the multitude came together, and were confused, because everyone heard them speak in his own language.*

As we take everything that has preceded this point in ministry—all of the fire and agreement and prophetically established plans of action—we can expect people to look at us with wild confusion. When it goes public, it will be a strange and unique invasion into their world. As we have discovered previously, we don't tone down the strange and wild flow of the Holy Spirit—we expect it to be turned up—way, way up!

A roadblock that we have unwittingly established in our pursuit of the development of the city church is that of relevance. We hear about the *emergent church* and being relevant in that context so it is easier for the lost to grasp the truth of God.

The problem? There is more than one. First, such a mindset presumes the culture of the world is somewhat normal and we must play catch up in order to more easily be understood and welcomed into that world. We forget that the world we are attempting to invite people into will totally shock their system! When they find the life of Jesus in a legitimate way they will be speaking in tongues, prophesying, dancing in the Spirit, praying without ceasing and exhibiting other wild behaviors. Also, we risk dumbing down the supernatural work of the Holy Spirit. The things of the Spirit must be discerned spiritually, yet we have become accustomed, even in our churches, to attempting to grasp and explain God intellectually.

Another problem is that we can greatly limit God. We try to put ourselves in the other person's shoes and then decide what type of ministry will be most appropriate for them. This is where the prophetic comes into play. It's incredibly important that we hear God, receive what he has for us and then pour out accordingly. For example, I once received a letter from a visitor to our church. He had a hard time believing we were so focused on worship, prayer, the prophetic, etc. He felt that the people of Manitou Springs would only respond to a seeker sensitive type of ministry. This person had a very narrow understanding of what the goal was and what it would take to accomplish it. I've heard it said that there have been fourteen churches in Manitou Springs since the 1980's that have started and failed within their first two years. This tells me something else must be done. A unique, earth-shaking, Holy Spirit driven move of God that heals, delivers and reveals the power of a tangible yet invisible Holy Force is needed here—just as in the days of the first church.

Yes, many will resist. Offense will come. But, so will the abundant life that only comes as we walk in the Spirit. Plus, it's important to remember the international focus. The mission here isn't only about the wonderful people of this city, but it's about the millions of others that will be affected as Manitou Springs becomes a power source for the nations.

In our various pursuits of establishing a city church, we must at this stage of the process be very clear and comfortable with the strategy of God. It will become easy to violate that strategy when demands and critiques start filling your email inbox. Keep in mind—new, apostolic moves of God have to be experienced first, then understood. Gideon's plan of action would have been mocked, opposed and murmured against. It made no sense at all—but it was the instruction of the Lord. Only he heard it, and he was responsible to obey all the way to completion. It's the same for us in these end-times.

## EVALUATION

Is there a unique, miraculous move of the Holy Spirit starting to pour into the streets? Is it counter cultural? Is it pure and holy and drawing attention to God? Is it slightly strange? Does it shock the local culture rather than affirm it? Be encouraged, you are well on your way to experiencing revival on a city level!

# ELEMENT SEVEN
## *A DECLARATION OF GOD'S WORKS*

*Acts 2:11 "Cretans and Arabs--we hear them speaking in our own tongues the wonderful works of God."*

You'll notice that up until this point in the establishment of the first church that there has been no mention of the ministries that we identify with the local church experience. No teaching, no evangelism, no Sunday School, no small groups. It hasn't been time for them. It has been premature to focus significantly that way.

Remember, the development of a church must be established on the presence of the Holy Spirit, prayer and an intensely prophetic focus. Everyone must be filled, endowed with power and boldness and ready to move out.

Here in verse eleven, which is really attached to verse six and the previous element, we see those who have received power begin to move out into society. They had something wonderful to give–and it wasn't knowledge, a formula for success or wonderful fellowship. It was entirely experience driven–yet it was undeniably God.

Those in the upper room experienced a new move of the Holy Spirit and they were simply spilling out everywhere they went! Note that it was a corporate outpouring and the result was a corporate ministry.

I can imagine based on the next element that they were so full of the power and life of the Holy Spirit that they were stumbling and groaning and stuttering and crying out as mad men and women!

It wasn't a teaching environment at this stage, but it was a time of declaration!

We can only imagine how wonderfully they shouted the experience they were having to the multitudes. They were zealots! Fanatics! Revolutionaries! They were communicating the substance of an invisible God through a life-changing experience with Him! It's something you can't put into words, but I am certain of this–the words that were used, coupled with the zeal and body language and boldness that was all over these people, shook that great city to its core.

I contend that we better not move into large scale strategic ministry until we have what they had! We need to see into an awe inspiring invisible realm where God is stirring so we can effectively transmit that to others. It was once said by an unknown person,

> *People of vision see the invisible, hear the inaudible, believe the incredible, think the unthinkable and do the impossible!*

If we are to introduce the amazing yet invisible realities of God to a lost and spiritually numb society, we better be highly sensitive and very well acquainted with that realm. When we peer into that realm, we simply cannot maintain our emotionless and dignified position of status-quo!

> *2 Samuel 6:22 "And I will be even more undignified than this, and will be humble in my own sight. But as for the maidservants of whom you have spoken, by them I will be held in honor."*

I heard someone say recently that we need PhD's in the pulpits again so we can learn the deep truths of scripture. As long as those people are in a place of deep, intimate and wild prayer every day of their lives, then bring on the doctors!

But, if they are not, I'd rather listen to someone who is one day old in the Lord and burning in zeal. A person who just came through the fire of the Holy Spirit has much more to say than any theologian who bases his ministry on knowledge alone.

Allow me to make an important point here. This is the very reason why we don't want to prematurely launch a public ministry. We don't want to introduce people into a logical or even emotional lifestyle of religious activity. The salvation experience must be one of just that–Holy Spirit driven experience in the furnace of prayer. The job of the evangelist is not to cause people to repeat a prayer and come to church. His job is to introduce people to God Himself. That's why evangelists must be people of deep prayer. Their goal is to take the lost by the hand and lead them right into the prayer room where the Living God is burning through them! These people will crave to pray without ceasing!

We can grow churches through good programs, good teaching and other attempts. But, the coming reformation that is being mapped out in this book will shake all of that down to a place of raw hunger, prayer and experiential encounters with God day after day after day.

When we find ourselves on our faces in tears and without words to effectively share what just happened after being caught up and emblazoned by the power of Almighty God we'll know we have something well worth communicating.

## EVALUATION

Is the experience in your core group so overwhelming that it is starting to shake your city? Is everybody in the church corporately full of this outpouring of God? Is the DNA of your local body so powerful and unique that it causes eyebrows to raise? Is everything taking a back seat to the experience and impartation of the Holy Spirit? Are you writing down all of the amazing occurrences of God in your meetings? Do you perceive that the local culture is now threatened by the Holy Spirit? Can you see your entire city being a dwelling place of the Holy Spirit? If so, get ready–great resistance is at hand! Read on.

# E L E M E N T   E I G H T

*THE EXTREME NATURE OF MINISTRY WILL CAUSE SOME TO*

*MARVEL AND SOME TO MOCK*

---

*Acts 2:12-13 So they were all amazed and perplexed, saying to one another, "Whatever could this mean?" Others mocking said, "They are full of new wine."*

This is where the rubber meets the road. Do you see now why an attempt at relevancy at this point actually works against the biblical flow of church development?

If what happened in the previous element was as earth-shaking as it should have been, then what will be experienced in this element will be a great evidence of being on track.

You will start to see people coming to you with extreme excitement on their faces. I'm talking about both Christians and non-Christians. These people will be thrilled to have found someone who has the guts to initiate true reformation. The flow of the Holy Spirit will be amazing and people's lives will be tangibly touched in dramatic ways.

However, you must prepare yourself for great resistance–again from both Christians and non-Christians.  It will possibly be the very people that you crave affirmation from that will distance themselves from you.

> *Matthew 5:10-12 Blessed are those who are persecuted for righteous-*
> *ness' sake, For theirs is the kingdom of heaven. "Blessed are you when*
> *they revile and persecute you, and say all kinds of evil against you*
> *falsely for My sake. Rejoice and be exceedingly glad, for great is your*
> *reward in heaven, for so they persecuted the prophets who were before*
> *you."*

When traditional religion is invaded with a John the Baptist type of prophetic offense, those who make their livings from the current system will often resist.  Others who truly have a good heart, but are wired differently and have a lack of understanding of the new move of God will often feel you have abandoned 'old time religion' that has been a staple for years.

It's at this phase that we must remain deeply prayerful, humble, full of love and life, bold and confident that God has indeed called us to partici-pate in a brand new move of the Lord.  The new wine of God's new move will make most uncomfortable, and it would do us well to understand this early on.

While it may be a very lonely place at times, it's important to stay close to God and to others.  Pray God gives you some significant relationships with people who share your DNA.  They will be precious friends to say the least.

It's at this stage of the game where it seems that many ministries should be launching in the church and you may receive pressure to start them.  Be very careful here!  For example, as Revolution was transitioning into this process as a house of prayer, there was the challenge for everybody to be saturated in the Holy Spirit.  Everybody needed to be in position to receive regular impartation directly from God.  Our traditional teach-ing services took a back seat to an atmosphere of contending for God to manifest in us.  This was in direct response to a heavy mandate from the Lord, yet there were a few who simply could not understand this strategy.  And, guess what—they were gifted as teachers!

The thought that their personal gifts and desires needed to be re-prioritized in the corporate model of ministry and laid aside (to a degree) for a season cause great offense.

You will find people making demands on you at times, especially when it comes to a seeming lack of focus on their favorite gift or office in the body. Do you have the courage to hear God and obey His every directive even in the face of accusation or resistance?

Here is a critical and possibly ministry saving truth—if accusation starts to rise up in your ministry, you simply know the enemy is at play. Whether there is some truth to it or not, a spirit of accusation craves to be embraced by those in the body—and when brothers and sisters are offended, the spirit of accusation is often called on to help in the mission to resist.

It's important that we understand this point clearly, and I'm purposely focusing on it in a very intentional way. You must discover the wonderful place of loving people deeply even in the midst of accusation and abandonment. Additionally, you must know that you know that God is leading you. He loves you!

*Matthew 27:12 And while He was being accused by the chief priests and elders, He answered nothing.*

Jesus simply loved—all the way to the cross.

*1 Peter 3:15-17 But sanctify the Lord God in your hearts, and always be ready to give a defense to everyone who asks you a reason for the hope that is in you, with meekness and fear; having a good conscience, that when they defame you as evildoers, those who revile your good conduct in Christ may be ashamed. For it is better, if it is the will of God, to suffer for doing good than for doing evil.*

Certainly be ready to share with people why you are moving in the direction you are, but avoid debate. Avoid the desire to prove yourself right. Simply move ahead in obedience, love and as a healthy and humble leader.

My wife and I went through quite a process when we decided to take Revolution into the deep as a ministry of prayer. I'll wear my emotions on my sleeve here in order for you to have a clear picture of what we went through and what you might expect. Of course, I pray that your pursuit is free of any resistance at all!

Something I still struggle with to this day is the reality that most people will only participate in ministry if they are getting something out of it. If they are able to minister according to their gift mix, then they believe they can be very happy. But, as challenge increased and there was great need of a season of intense unity we were disappointed to find that some weren't willing to respond. Our unity at that phase of ministry was lacking. *I realized that some great people who love Jesus very much simply weren't devoted to the fulfillment of the vision that God had given me in 1991–to take a city for Jesus.*

Isn't the mission of ushering in revival in Manitou Springs in such a way that millions of people's lives are changed around the world worth dying for? That question would resound in my spirit night and day. Isn't the vision clear? It's worth setting everything aside for, right?

God had given me one of the most significant strategic visions of our ministry's history a few years ago. The vision unfolded in my spirit as a blueprint of a house. I asked an artist to draw it for me. The vision was of a mansion which had a huge main area. This area was consumed with fire. People were there on their face in the presence of the fire of God night and day. I then saw them, one by one, stand up, literally consumed in fire, and run to another room, and then back again into the fire. They were themselves on fire as they ran, and they took that fire into their room. The room represented their ministry assignment.

There is much more to it than that, but for the sake of space, allow me to explain the process that was to be initiated. According to the vision, we were all to be in a place of zealous prayer many hours a week at Revolution. Not just intercessors or prayer warriors–every single person just as in Acts chapter two. Then, as we were consumed with the resulting fire we would all run according to the giftings and callings on our lives in great unity with a common goal before us. Some would teach, others would lead small groups and others would evangelize. It made a lot of sense and was very easy to understand–so I thought.

I was saddened and shocked that most wanted to hurdle the 'prayer part' and simply assume their place of ministry. Sure, they were willing to go through leadership classes and do as good a job as they could in their roles. These truly were wonderful people with great hearts.

But, why no prayer? Yes, some stepped into the prayer room, but many did not. Keep in mind that I had been teaching on prayer nearly non-stop for years. So, as time went by I realized we were attempting an improper advance without the necessary fire of prayer on a corporate or personal level. We could maintain, but we simply could not advance appropriately. God had us transition completely into a house of prayer–a house of fire. An upper room. Most programs were eliminated so we could hit our faces and cry out for God to consume us. God knew that we were not able to accomplish such an international mission on the level of power and corporate pursuit that we

*An artist's rendition of the House of Dreams vision I had*

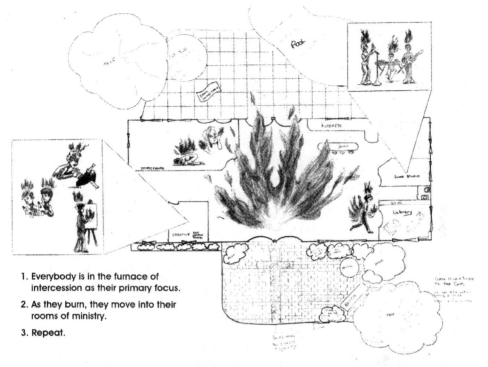

1. Everybody is in the furnace of intercession as their primary focus.
2. As they burn, they move into their rooms of ministry.
3. Repeat.

had. The cry of desperation had to be found again.

At this point a great purging came to our ministry. It was easily the most difficult, lonely and painful season of tears that my wife and I had ever experienced in the ministry—but it was also the most necessary and important season.

My wife's and my test was at least two fold:

1. Would we obey God's strategy even in the face of pain?
2. Would we discover the joy of praying huge blessings on those who hurt us and abandoned the mission?

While it was a process, and we often felt like we got hit by a bus—every day for weeks at a time, we passed the test. We had no choice but to remain obedient and pure of heart. Both God and the devil were at play in the situation. God allowed much to happen to cause purging, breaking and strengthening in the church and also to test our hearts. The enemy disoriented people and removed them from their place of responsibility.

Additionally, in the same season of trial, many residents and business owners in the city were very upset that we were praying about revival here. I received countless emails–from the leader of the Masonic Lodge, witches, residents and others–even as far away as Egypt! The City Council was nervous about our mission and visited us. The newspaper interviewed me–all because we were praying!

Do you see how a focus on an upper room atmosphere brought great offense both to those in the church and those who don't even believe in prayer? The spiritual, invisible atmosphere was filled with activity, and people didn't know how to handle it.

As you proceed in the power of the Holy Spirit, you will make mistakes, you will struggle at times, Christians will turn on you, non-Christians will mock you–and revival will come!

Amy and I, as well as the other faithful fire-breathers at Revolution House of Prayer, have found some amazing friends and are experiencing God at a degree we could never have imagined in our past seasons as a traditional American style church.

While we are far from perfect, and we make mistakes as we venture into the unknown, one thing can be said–we love God with passion. We also love those who have been with us in the past–and we are so excited to have seen some return. Some were released into other great local churches and are doing very well. It is so important to have an offense free heart and a love for everyone in our lives. As we do, God will be able to facilitate some powerful moves in and through us.

As this happens, both marveling and mocking will come. The enemy will do anything to bottleneck the flow of God in a ministry. There are many telltale signs that this is happening. Become well acquainted with God's proper process for dispute resolution within a body. When you see a violation of that process, you can be assured the enemy is behind or at least deeply involved in the activity.

For example, if you ever hear complaining or murmuring, you know the devil has grabbed on.

*Philippians 2:14 Do all things without complaining and disputing,*

Gossip is another activity that is forbidden by God. I have shared that any discussion that includes disagreement, frustration or irritation about a third party is witchcraft. It's gossip. That's why it's so critical that as a leader we never murmur about others. We cannot accuse them. If we embrace those spirits, they will one day turn on us!

So, stay pure, humble, holy and without offense. Expect disagreement and persecution from within the ranks and also from those in the city. Stand firm in your resolve to lead from a position of obedience to God and not man. But, also expect great marveling at the new move of God that is being poured out!

## EVALUATION

At this point, you will most certainly be experiencing a deeper revelation of many realities in the pursuit of Kingdom advance in your city. The extreme nature of your lifestyle and resulting ministry will cause a remnant to get extremely excited. You should have miraculous testimonies and other reportable moves of God to talk about. You most probably have had encounters with a variety of opposing spirits—Absalom, Jezebel, and a myriad of others. You will be graded on how you handled these encounters. Did offense take root? Did love prevail? Did the fear of man cause you to lose focus or did you stay on track? Are you both humble and bold? Broken and burning? If so, you are effectively maturing—and God is ready to use you to proclaim the very Word that will result in a great harvest. If you are struggling, stop here. Take a prayer and fasting trip. Pray for those who have hurt you. Cry out for God to help you grow through this stage. It's critical to learn how to navigate this phase, because it will present itself time and time again as you advance.

# ELEMENT NINE
## *PREACHING & EXPLAINING THE MOVE OF THE HOLY SPIRIT*

*Acts 2:15-16 For these are not drunk, as you suppose, since it is only the third hour of the day. But this is what was spoken by the prophet Joel:*

Many desire to launch their ministry here–proclaiming to the masses the wonderful works of Jesus in the hopes that they get saved and start coming to church. There are several problems with this mindset. Of course, there is nothing wrong with being zealous to complete our mission, but we must use wisdom. There is a process.

In this element, Peter wasn't simply giving a Bible lesson. What was he doing, then?

To attempt to start a ministry at this point doesn't make sense when we understand the scenario Peter was ministering in. He was using the unique move of God that exploded out of the upper room as an opportunity to explain it and the Kingdom of God to everybody who witnessed it.

So, when revival has broken out, and God is showing up in an unusual way, we will have the opportunity to teach and explain all that is happening to those who are listening. Of course, the chance to build upon and expand into other scriptural elements will present itself in a powerful way.

At Revolution, we have two perspectives when it comes to teaching:

1. **Pre-revival**–teach everything we can to advance the idea of revival. A sermon that I am teaching now is, "The Lifestyle of a Forerunner". The basic idea is that if we want revival later, we must model revival now. What will we be doing when revival breaks out? Practically and spiritually? Do that now.
2. **During revival**–Boundless opportunities will exist to explain everything from manifestations of God's presence to evangelism to repentance to tithing. Such teachings will take root easily in a revival atmosphere.

So, the basic idea is this–the high majority of teaching before revival breaks out must be on topics that directly lead to the experience of revival. This book is a great example of pre-revival teaching. This is a manual of revival that fits well in a pre-revival setting. This is why it is so important that your *upper room team* is entirely focused on the goal. If you have people in the mix that desire other things (other good things, but things that are outside of the current strategic focus), you will find disunity start to arise.

Then, when revival breaks out, the people and the teaching atmosphere is ready for a great expanse of the scope of impartation. A Holy Spirit driven atmosphere causes the wide range of biblical topics that need to be addressed to be infused with great staying power.

> *1 John 2:27 But the anointing which you have received from Him abides in you, and you do not need that anyone teach you; but as the same anointing teaches you concerning all things, and is true, and is not a lie, and just as it has taught you, you will abide in Him.*

It's in a Holy Spirit driven atmosphere where the teaching anointing exists. In this environment the Holy Spirit will be imparting revelation to the masses through any number of experiential manifestations–and then, the teacher will simply declare and explain what the Holy Spirit has already initiated.

This is why in most churches today we will experience a musical worship set prior to the teaching of the Word. There is an innate understanding of the need for the Holy Spirit to be invited, stirred and heeded in order for teaching to be of any effect. Of course, this simple structure is far from what God has planned for those who seek revival. The entire experience from beginning to end will be that of extreme worship, prayer and the fire of teaching.

An easy way to say it is that the experiential much more easily translates into information than the other way around. Knowledge, or information, that starts in the mind has a very difficult time making it into our spirits.

To be scorched by the Holy Spirit in a place of lengthy prayer will result in some amazing truths being experienced. It's in this place of prayer where we will *know God* instead of simply *knowing about Him*.

I often ask people, if they were on the moon, would they rather learn about oxygen or experience oxygen? Both are good. Both are important. But which is most important? We could try to learn about the makeup of oxygen– for about sixty seconds. Then we'd simply die as we pursue knowledge. This is far to common in the church today. We must breath the air of the Spirit and allow our knowledge to come directly from our encounter with Him.

As we experience the Rhema revelation of God, we will be able to support it easily with a myriad of powerful scriptures. Our personal and undeniable experience coupled with the Living Word of God (the Logos) will result in deeply penetrating and life altering teaching.

*Romans 10:17 So then faith comes by hearing, and hearing by the word of God.*

The word 'word' in this passage comes from the Greek word, "Rhema". It's the experiential revelation that causes people to believe, not an intellectual understanding of the written Word. It's in the place of experiential prayer where both the Rhema and the Logos explode into people. This is the goal of this element–to experience God in a powerful way and then impart that to others.

We're developing an internship program at RHOP as I write this. I am training my leaders to get ready to impart what they have experienced with God into these new interns–support it with scripture, with testimonies and with other powerful mediums. But, don't 'freak out' at the thought of 'teaching'. Simply pour out what has been poured into you. That's New Testament style teaching!

*Matthew 7:28-29  And so it was, when Jesus had ended these sayings, that the people were astonished at His teaching, for He taught them as one having authority, and not as the scribes.*

## EVALUATION

Simply ask yourself if what you are teaching is being fueled by what the Holy Spirit has initiated or not.  Are you teaching pre-revival material or is your content coming from what the revival atmosphere demands?  If it's the latter, then you are right on track.  If it is the former, then you are probably still somewhere on the time line prior to element six.

# ELEMENT TEN
## PROPHECIES, DREAMS & VISIONS

*Acts 2:17-18 'And it shall come to pass in the last days, says God, That I will pour out of My Spirit on all flesh; Your sons and your daughters shall prophesy, Your young men shall see visions, Your old men shall dream dreams. And on My menservants and on My maidservants I will pour out My Spirit in those days; And they shall prophesy.'*

I find it interesting that the first sermon that the people heard was one on the extreme supernatural. Most beginner classes, or pre-Believer messages, seem to stay far and wide of any such focus. However, the first church was birthed supernaturally without apology.

*Galatians 3:2-5 This only I want to learn from you: Did you receive the Spirit by the works of the law, or by the hearing of faith? Are you so foolish? Having begun in the Spirit, are you now being made perfect by the flesh? Have you suffered so many things in vain--if indeed it was in vain? Therefore He who supplies the Spirit to you and works miracles among you, does He do it by the works of the law, or by the hearing of faith?*

They began in the Spirit. Our churches must be birthed in the Spirit and full of Holy Spirit activity, miracles and great power.

We hear much about relevance, avoiding the use of church language and other ideas that would seem to make it easier for the unbeliever to get saved. Peter, however, was in the middle of a wild, Holy Spirit driven environment. The supernatural was being revealed in a substantial and phenomenal way. To ignore what God was doing would result in working contrary to the plan and structure of the church.

It's at this point that established church leaders must consider a question. While you may be experiencing church growth and even new conversions, are people being birthed into what this element presents? Are they presented with the extreme challenge of a prayer filled and supernatural life as a part of their introduction into your church? If not, take some time and reconsider the innate power of your current structure. Remember, the goal is for every Believer, new and mature, to pray hours a day, to be full of the Holy Spirit, to be together continually and, as we'll discuss further in this element, to prophesy, dream and have visions on a regular basis.

> John 10:27 My sheep hear My voice, and I know them, and they follow Me.

I teach on this idea a lot–every Believer simply must discover how to hear God's voice! In another book I wrote titled *Revelation Driven Prayer*, I discuss this idea in great length. It shocks me how many people simply don't hear God.

I was speaking at a conference on the topic of *Revelation Driven Prayer* and I asked a question: "How many of you have never heard God?"

I explained what this meant as I was asking the question. I spoke on prophecy, visions, dreams and other modes of communication that God uses. Approximately 90% of those who were there admitted that they have never heard God.

I often present the question to people when discussing the present voice of the Holy Spirit: "If you don't hear God, how do you know at any given moment in your day what you should do, where you should go, what you are to pray for or what specific instructions God has for you?"

If we are truly experiencing the Holy Spirit in the magnitude that the first church did, many will spontaneously begin receiving visions, having dreams and experiencing God in a very clear way. This is why Peter was teaching on it. The Holy Spirit had arrived on the scene and it was important to teach on a critical element of His function.

In order for the first church to expand as it did, clear and present communication from God had to be a normal and expected part of every participant's life.

> *Acts 21:4 And finding disciples, we stayed there seven days. They told Paul through the Spirit not to go up to Jerusalem.*

We see clear and present instruction coming from the Holy Spirit in this verse. Without that insight, they would have had to resort to good old common sense, which many more times than not will result in missing God's perfect will.

> *Acts 21:11 When he had come to us, he took Paul's belt, bound his own hands and feet, and said, "Thus says the Holy Spirit, 'So shall the Jews at Jerusalem bind the man who owns this belt, and deliver him into the hands of the Gentiles.'"*

The Holy Spirit again gives insight on what is to come. It is so important that we allow God to prepare and test our hearts for certain trying events that will soon come. This comes through dreams, visions and other forms of revelation. Again, to be void of this revelation would cause us to be ill prepared and to move, at times, in directions contrary to what God wants.

Take a look at a scripture in the first chapter of Acts. Of course, this takes place just prior to the arrival of the Holy Spirit. I wonder how differently this decision would have been made after the Holy Spirit had arrived.

> *Acts 1:24-26 And they prayed and said, "You, O Lord, who know the hearts of all, show which of these two You have chosen to take part in this ministry and apostleship from which Judas by transgression fell, that he might go to his own place." And they cast their lots, and the lot fell on Matthias. And he was numbered with the eleven apostles.*

Does this process look very similar to a typical prayer in a Believer's life today? They had only a mandate—to fill the spot left by Judas. There was a need, yet there was no supernatural direction regarding the person the spot should be filled with. They prayed a prayer that is typical of most that are offered in the present day, "Oh Lord, may your will be done. I pray that your perfect plan comes to pass. Amen."

That type of prayer results in the casting of lots! We'll flip a coin and hope for the best!

What if the Holy Spirit had been in the midst of that meeting and specifically through dreams, visions or prophetic revelation told them who to pick?

No casting of lots, no guessing, no hoping for the best. As we understand that the church must embrace and teach this principle, we'll discover that the level of supernatural activity increases radically in our churches.

Everything from evangelism to giving of offerings to small group ministry will suddenly have very different results, very different focuses and very different power to run on. Now, the evangelist isn't simply knocking on a door and handing someone a tract, but they are coming out of the furnace of prayer and prophetically revealing to the cashier at the grocery store the message that God has for her at that very moment!

I once heard a story of a person who was at a shopping center. This person understood what it was to hear God–and God gave her an instruction that would never be found in an evangelism training course. God said, "I want you to stand on your head in the corner of the store."

What? From what I understand, this person wrestled with this directive considerably. I know I would have! Finally, she obeyed and stood on her head.

I can only imagine the resulting reactions that this brought. Laughter? No. Tears? Yes. A cashier approached this obedient servant of the Living God. She was crying and, after pulling herself together, told her that she just had prayed a prayer several minutes ago.

I asked God to prove that he loved me by having someone stand on their head.

No casting of lots or drawing of straws would have resulted in this amazing testimony. We simply have to teach people how to hear God.

What if God wanted a ministry to purchase a one million dollar piece of property. God knew that they would need the space for a great harvest in their city. And, what if God designated ten people to each give $100,000. If any less than 100% of those people heard the Rhema directive of God to sow into the ministry in that way, the mission would be greatly compromised. We all must hear God, and Peter was sharing that this important missional element must be received by all involved.

# EVALUATION

At this point all of your original team members must be flowing easily in the prophetic. If this is not the case, something has been neglected. However, if you are truly at this element, so much unusual activity of the Holy Spirit will be manifesting that you will have no choice but to explain the amazing reality of the invisible realm to everybody involved. Do you feel you are mature in the understanding of the supernatural? Are you teaching it well? Is the hunger for the miraculous increasing at a great rate? Are you comfortable bringing in new Believers at this point? Do you understand that you cannot 'tone it down' for the sake of the masses? The result of the explosion of spiritual hunger is salvation. You are about to receive an influx of new Believers who will quickly become experts in the invisible realm of the Holy Spirit. I often tell people in my ministry—make sure you are so strong, mature and acquainted with the activity of the Holy Spirit that the incoming new Believers don't fly right past you! Their hunger will have the strength of a nuclear explosion.

# ELEMENT ELEVEN

## *THE PREACHING OF SALVATION*

*Acts 2:21 'And it shall come to pass That whoever calls on the name of the Lord Shall be saved.'*

Now, 21 verses and possibly months or years into the process, the masses are ready. Do you realize that it may take your new church an extreme amount of time to make it to this point? If you have an established church, it may take even longer to destruct and reconstruct.

We need to keep in mind that we are embracing a city church model. I don't believe we can realistically expect a single department to bear the weight of the coming harvest. Entire local churches will need to become specialists and narrow their focus to a single area.

As the preaching of salvation begins to resound in the city, there will be a few central locations for that preaching to be heard. As people flood into this place—it may even be a park or amphitheater in the city—that particular place must be free to focus entirely on the influx of people as the preaching of salvation goes out. This place will have strong apostolic leadership in place along with evangelists and other outreach gifted individuals.

This department of the city church, though it will consist of entire properties that used to function as local churches, will focus almost entirely on preaching, revival and evangelism. Of course, there is flexibility as to the exact makeup of offices in this department, but it will be outreach focused.

And, don't forget, in another part of town the most important ministry of all has now been going night and day for a long time–the house of prayer. So, 24 hours a day people are in the house of prayer ministering to God, interceding for the city church, for leaders and for nations. The leaders of the newly formed *preaching department* are in the house of prayer many hours a week, and most usually, every day.

So, after all of this time, the city church now has two departments! The house of prayer and the preaching center which is made up of mostly apostles and evangelists.

Both departments are led by strong apostolic people who have responsibility on a city level.

The fire in the house of prayer led to an outpouring of the Holy Spirit which led to the need to explain all that God was doing. This led to a ripe harvest–people who were hungry for the supernatural presence of God to consume their lives.

The house of prayer must continue with great intensity. It's the most important department in the city church. So goes the house of prayer, so goes the mission. Every department must remain connected daily to the house of prayer. The apostolic leadership in the city must govern well and ensure every leader and every new Believer is burning with the fire that's found in the place of continual prayer.

> *Leviticus 6:13 A fire shall always be burning on the altar; it shall never go out.*

## EVALUATION

Do you have a good understanding of the city church model? Do you see the natural expansion from a house of prayer model to a second city church department? Who are the apostolic leaders of the city? Who is in charge of the house of prayer? Are there actually people ready to receive the preaching of salvation? If not, then keep praying. Keep stirring the atmosphere. You need much more Holy Spirit supernatural activity. If people are responding, move on to element twelve. A move of holiness is about to erupt.

# ELEMENT TWELVE
## *REPENTANCE*

*Acts 2:38 Then Peter said to them, "Repent, and let every one of you be baptized in the name of Jesus Christ for the remission of sins; and you shall receive the gift of the Holy Spirit."*

This step should flow naturally out of what everybody has experienced thus far. An extreme move of the Holy Spirit simply results in a great fear of God, a craving of holiness and a continually repentant heart.

The difference between the lost and those who are flowing in the Spirit of revival will be extreme—more so than black and white. An unapologetic call to holiness, repentance and hunger for the purity of God will consume the atmosphere.

A radical John the Baptist type of call will resound:

*Repent! The Kingdom of God is at hand!*

This is not a seeker sensitive movement at all—but quite the opposite. It's aggressive, confrontational and prophetic. The previous preparation of the atmosphere that started picking up speed in verse one of Acts chapter two will result in and demand nothing less than a declaration of death to self, the embracing of a bloody cross and the brokenness of a desperate soul as he looks upon the face of Jesus.

We often hear about revivals of old that resulted in bars closing, crime dissipating and other very tangible marks of transformation. It's repentance and the hunger for holiness that will cause this to happen—nothing less.

Repentance is one of the most beautiful words I know. In that word is the blessed assurance that God actually craves for us to be with Him! We can cry out for our Father with tears in our eyes and he will run to us!

It should be clear at this point why such an extreme process of prayer and the infusion of the Holy Spirit is so necessary. We cannot expect to launch a revival or a city church at this point! We must go through the process of Holy Spirit fire before we can ever expect to participate in a movement of God to this degree. Everything prior to this element has prepared us not only to participate in revival, but to lead it. We will with confidence be able to look at the masses and say, "Follow me as I follow Christ."

## EVALUATION

Do you truly understand the magnitude of this phase of ministry? Is a craving for holiness burning in your veins? Can you confidently tell someone as Paul did, "Follow me as I follow Christ"? Is the atmosphere hot enough that people are running to the altars? Is the message they are responding to one of death on a cross? Would you say that you really are experiencing the beginnings of an earth-shaking revival of biblical proportions? Well done! Get ready to experience potentially the greatest explosion of Holy Spirit power in generations!

# ELEMENT THIRTEEN

## GIFT OF THE HOLY SPIRIT & POWER ENCOUNTERS

*Acts 2:38 Then Peter said to them, "Repent, and let every one of you be baptized in the name of Jesus Christ for the remission of sins; and you shall receive the gift of the Holy Spirit."*

This is such an important element to understand. Just as with the original *upper room team*, every new Believer will receive the impartation of the Holy Spirit.

This is one reason that it is extremely critical that every original team member is filled. That team will be responsible for the baptism of power that will be experienced in countless lives as the influx of new Believers intensifies.

I heard someone preach a long time ago on the baptism of the Holy Spirit. He said something like, "You don't want someone who hasn't been baptized in the Holy Spirit to teach on the baptism of the Holy Spirit!"

The first church, and the emerging city churches that are in the earliest of stages now, were and are dependant on the movement of the Holy Spirit in individual's lives. The advance of the Kingdom of God is a supernatural advance, and thus requires people who are uniquely acquainted with supernatural activities. In the Western world primarily, we tend to function from the intellect and emotions almost exclusively. Concepts, formulas, principles and structures that can be reported, repeated and transferred logically are what most church planters, pastors and other leaders tend to gravitate toward.

Church consultants, church growth books, conferences and other helps are readily available. Certainly, there are principles that are quite helpful, though what God wants to do in a ministry goes well beyond what can be captured intellectually.

An elementary and non-negotiable element for church growth, city transformation and a visitation of the Holy Spirit is extreme supernatural activity. To assume we can expect transformation to result from a ministry that is based on human understanding alone is unrealistic.

There are over 19,000 cities in the United States, and as of this writing none of them are experiencing revival. This means the strategies that are being implemented by churches and ministries in cities from coast to coast are not having the appropriate results. Certainly many good things are being done and many lives are being touched by God in some amazing churches across the nation, but would it be safe to say that there must be more? Much more?

As we learn to become dependant on the overwhelming supernatural activity of the Holy Spirit in the invisible realm, we will venture into arenas never before even considered. We will discover that our mission is far beyond what our human capacity can serve. Every day we will become reliant on:

- Prophetic revelation
- Praying in tongues
- Hearing God clearly
- Supernatural boldness and power
- Dreams and visions
- Discerning of spirits
- Deliverance
- Spiritual warfare

As God presents His seeming impossible missions to us, we will become desperate for Him to reveal His specific revelation to us. Power encounters in our cities will be expected and we'll have the ability to be victorious in them. The anointing that resonates from us will be stunning to those we meet.

Those saved in the mission will quickly become fellow soldiers in the battle—and they will simply need to have the ability to navigate the invisible realm. Survival, much less personal and corporate advance, will depend on it.

This is a primary church growth and Kingdom advance strategy. The supernatural activity around every Believer must be intense and continual. To live without this, without dreams and visions, without prophecy, without power and boldness, will result in frustration, a well below average life and an unfulfilled mission. Simply, what God has called each of us to cannot be fulfilled without the fire of the Holy Spirit burning very hot.

This is why the primary structure in the city church, and in a local church, must be the house of prayer. That fire must NEVER go out, and it must be attended to continually. If people are attempting to minister without being people of extreme and continual prayer—they will fail. An elementary and primary activity of every Believer absolutely must be lengthy and fervent intercession. We as leaders have dropped the ball time and again by not praying in this fashion ourselves, and in turn by not holding those under our care accountable.

## EVALUATION

As people are responding to a salvation message, are you focused on ensuring that each is filled with the Holy Spirit? Many churches will funnel new Believers into a small group, which is not a bad idea at all. But, these new Believers must also be funneled into the house of prayer. Do you have a system of integrating people into a place of enjoyable yet fervent prayer? Is the bar for each new Believer high enough to ensure they understand the wild commitment that the Christian life demands? Are you ready to ensure they understand the wonderful importance of flowing in prophecy, dreams, visions, healing and other supernatural functions? If so, now it's time for the church to grow!

# ELEMENT FOURTEEN
## *GROWTH*

*Acts 2:42 And they continued steadfastly in the apostles' doctrine and fellowship, in the breaking of bread, and in prayers.*

You've arrived at element fourteen. I assume you have been introduced to a fresh understanding of what must happen prior to making it to this point. The process is extreme! It may take years to make it this far, yet so many churches attempt to launch from this place instead of appropriately stepping through God's prescribed process.

After looking at the extreme diligence one must possess to get to this point, the idea of attempting to start a church from this point makes little sense. The foundational work of the Holy Spirit must come first.

Now it's time to teach! Why? There are new soldiers awaiting their instructions. Up until this point, the *upper room team* was made up of maturing and intensely focused people. While there should certainly be an element of training at that stage, it will be very narrowly focused. In the early stages the upper room team training sessions are more like strategy meetings than traditional teaching services. You teach on what you need to accomplish in the next mission. People at that phase should be encouraged to be self-starters and to intentionally grow in other disciplines through reading books, prayer, listen to sermon CD's, etc. This is important so as not to cause deviation from the very narrow focus of the corporate team.

But now, in this element, there are new Believers that need to be equipped, so bring on the teachers! There is a brand new introduction to a wonderful family of Believers, so open up the small groups. Pastors, are you ready to shepherd?

Prior to making it to this element, it's very important to have the right people in position awaiting the influx of new Believers. It's here in verse 42 where it becomes critical for teachers, pastors and others uniquely equipped to nurture, train and release to be ready to serve.

Growth on a personal and small group level will result in growth on a much larger scale. The expected lifestyle of Believers had been modeled well by the 120 in the launch team, and now they will have a great and challenging time imparting that lifestyle into their new friends.

Many will be pouring into many. The amazing truths of the Word of God will explode out of the team and will be soaked up by everybody else.

It may seem like the supernatural activity of the Holy Spirit is de-emphasized in this phase, but whatever you do, don't allow this to happen! Not only must this phase result in a school of learning, it must be a school of burning!

Gather together the flock and teach them to be fire-breathers! Training in everything from prayer to the prophetic to holiness to who they are in Christ must be continual here.

In the city church there will be at least one specific department that will most probably be open several hours every day for training. Every Believer in the city will be involved in classes and other training opportunities. A person who holds the office of teacher will be responsible for the development of this department in accordance with the vision of the apostolic leadership they serve under.

So, on Mondays, while other people are in other departments of the city church (house of prayer, evangelism department, youth department, etc.), many people will be in class learning about prophecy. On Tuesdays, others will have the opportunity to discover their spiritual gifts, and on and on through the rest of the week. Every person should be enrolled in continual education in preparation for their Kingdom assignments.

## EVALUATION

Do you have an entire department readied for this important phase of ministry?  Who are your teachers?  What will they be teaching?  Are you sure it's time to launch into this element, or are you putting the cart before the horse?  Are there new Believers ready to be trained?  Or, are the seasoned Believers mishandling their personal responsibility to grow largely independently and thus increasing the demand on teachers?  Is the teaching geared for those who are ready to be equipped for ministry?  What expectations are there for growth and the assuming of ministry assignments?

# E L E M E N T   F I F T E E N
## *FELLOWSHIP*

*Acts 2:42 And they continued steadfastly in the apostles' doctrine and fellowship, in the breaking of bread, and in prayers.*

I often find this element a bit difficult to appropriately prioritize and define for people. We all crave a healthy social environment, and therefore this desire often causes us to misplace it in our order of priorities. First, fellowship is an important and fulfilling aspect of the Christian experience. However, fellowship was not designed to be, nor is it strong enough to be a foundational element. Fellowship simply cannot even come close to supporting the extreme weight of a missional church structure.

In the beginning of this book we saw that unity was mission driven as opposed to purely relationship driven. Consider the difference between extreme unity and simple fellowship:

> **Unity**–Christian people of all types agree on a common goal. The goal is so extreme that everybody understands that unity and submission to leadership simply are non-negotiables. These people may or

may not thoroughly enjoy spending time together, but they respect each other's strengths and callings. These people work feverishly through issues, obstacles and struggles so as to ensure the mission is not compromised.

**Fellowship**–Think pot-lucks and small groups. These are important elements of any growing church. While the point of unity is to pour out and support the cause, fellowship is a bit more driven by edification, intimacy and friendship. Simply, affinity groups develop naturally as people who enjoy one another spend time together. This is a wonderful part of the church, but, as has been said, it's not a foundational element. Contrarily, this element of fellowship is actually to be built on top of the previous foundational elements that we have discussed. Fellowship is driven on a variety of inner draws such as emotion, feeling, need, desire and at least a certain amount of discipline.

A church that considers this element to be their foundational strength is in great danger of constant scrutiny, division, emotional turmoil and church splits. Study the Absalom spirit and you will see how it can thrive in a system that is structurally based on fellowship.

However, a church that is strong otherwise can and should have a thriving social experience. We can't underestimate the importance of healthy community. Regularly gathering together throughout the week around the coffee table, on camp outs or in other small group settings is a natural expression of an emerging church. We need each other and should enjoy being together with God right in the middle of it all.

> *Ecclesiastes 4:9-12 Two are better than one, Because they have a good reward for their labor. For if they fall, one will lift up his companion. But woe to him who is alone when he falls, For he has no one to help him up. Again, if two lie down together, they will keep warm; But how can one be warm alone? Though one may be overpowered by another, two can withstand him. And a threefold cord is not quickly broken.*

As we start living life together in the heat of a New Testament revival atmosphere, it will be very important to be together often at a variety of levels, including socially. As we allow iron to sharpen iron on an interpersonal level the entire church will remain healthy and strong. We simply cannot assume that this element alone is sufficient to keep us pure and full of life. It's simply a result of a healthy church.

So, if you are starting a new church, don't expect this element to have any power at all to sustain a God-sized dream. But, have a plan ready to meet the social and relational needs and desires of people as they integrate into your growing church.

Another way to look at it is this:

It's unrealistic to presume a social structure can grow a church. To attend a conference on small group strategies and then attempt to implement that strategy with the expectation that church growth will suddenly explode is unrealistic. Small groups cannot be a propellent for explosive growth, but they can be a net to catch people who come in as a result of explosive growth.

As the other appropriately administered elements of church growth are effective, small groups must be in place to ensure people are well cared for.

So, this element can truly be a barometer of success. If you don't already have the power of God blazing through your church and city, you will have little need to progress beyond this point. It's not time for small group strategy yet. The people have no reason to show up and connect. But, when things do start to kick, look out! A lot of good old fashioned small groups, pot lucks and picnics will be happening every day and night in the city church!

## EVALUATION

A primary desire of most pastors is for people to love being together as they involve themselves in the ministry. This desire can bring with it great risks. If the extreme challenge and life-altering demands of a missional church experience haven't been emphasized and lived out for a significant amount of time, it can be tempting to compromise all of that for the sake of keeping happy people in the pews. Have you conquered this issue in your life? Will you contend aggressively and keep the bar of commitment very high even if it means you don't grow for ten or twenty years?

If you consider this a non-issue for you, and people are gathering together *in* the furnace of prayer and the presence of God, as opposed to simply gathering *around* that fire, then continue on. This next point will be the proof in the pudding.

# ELEMENT SIXTEEN
## *PRAYER*

*Acts 2:42 And they continued steadfastly in the apostles' doctrine and fellowship, in the breaking of bread, and in prayers.*

It's at this point that the idea of the city church becomes more clear. Remember, in one part of town (or for local churches, in one very large room) the 24/7 prayer house is burning hot. Every Believer, seasoned and brand new, will be frequenting that place on a daily basis.

Here's a critical barometer for you. If you have done a good job following God's original design for the launching of a church, you will see everybody in prayer all the time.

If you don't, there has been compromise and impatience somewhere previously in the process.

Again, let me state this very clearly–in the ancient and emerging model of the city church based on Acts chapter two, it will be absolutely normal for literally every person to be involved in ten, twenty or more hours of prayer every week! The prayer room should easily be overflowing 24 hours a day.

Due to the nature of the city church, most of these hours will be spent in the house of prayer. If you don't see this, something is terribly wrong, and you must have the courage to back up significantly. If someone doesn't have the overwhelming desire to be with God in intimate and passionate prayer on a continual basis, the core vision of the church was violated at some point.

Remember–the whole goal is to cause people to desperately crave and enjoy God. If we are filling our seats with lots of people who don't deeply desire God in prayer, it's a failed mission.

I find it sadly interesting that a majority of Christians shrink back when the topic of prayer is discussed. I believe we have done a poor job of explaining the idea of salvation to people. Saved people don't crave principles, ideas or methods for successful living. They desperately crave encounters with their Lover.

This is why the idea of developing a church outside of a expected flow of continual and desperate prayer doesn't calculate. God's church is a house of prayer. That's the definition of the church. A place to pray. If people are frequenting a church with out this being the dominant experience, we have tragically developed a system that is insufficient and significantly lacking.

So, it should simply be expected, based upon the DNA of the church, that every participant, member, new Believer and others connected with the ministry should be in deep prayer every day.

I believe it should be an untouchable rule that pastors and staff members spend at least 1/4th of their work day on their face in prayer. The results will be amazing.

> *Psalms 55:16-17 As for me, I will call upon God, And the Lord shall save me. Evening and morning and at noon I will pray, and cry aloud, And He shall hear my voice.*

> *Luke 6:12 Now it came to pass in those days that He went out to the mountain to pray, and continued all night in prayer to God.*

> *Acts 3:1 Now Peter and John went up together to the temple at the hour of prayer, the ninth hour.*

It's simply undeniable that the first church was birthed in prayer, continued in prayer, considered prayer to be the most important daily activity and actually had prescribed hours of prayer that were not violated.

This is the perfect place for a few quotes from a great revivalist, Leonard Ravenhill[1]:

*The tragedy of this late hour is that we have too many dead men in the pulpits giving out too many dead sermons to too many dead people....*

*Unction cannot be learned, only earned - by prayer...it is won or lost before the preacher's foot enters the pulpit.*

*The ugly fact is that altar fires are either out or burning very low. The prayer meeting is dead or dying. By our attitude to prayer we tell God that what was begun in the Spirit, we can finish in the flesh.*

And, my all time favorite quote that has burned in me for years:

*Ministers who do not spend two hours a day in prayer are not worth a dime a dozen, degrees or no degrees...Preachers who should be fishing for men are now too often fishing for compliments from men.*

Pastors! We must cancel our appointments, restructure our days and be on our face two or more hours every single day!

## EVALUATION

Take the pulse of your ministry. Would you say that everybody is an emerging expert on the topic of prayer? Do they crave God? Are most people experiencing dreams and visions on a regular basis? Do you have people coming to you regularly with prophetic insight that they received in prayer? Do you have 24/7 prayer up and running in your city? Is it a requirement for your leaders to spend hours a week in prayer? Simply, does everybody crave to experience God in a tangible way? If so, you are doing well. The next element will further prove whether you are on pace or out of alignment with the process.

1. Ravenhill, Leonard. *Why Revival Tarries*, Ada: Bethany House Publishers, 2004

# ELEMENT SEVENTEEN
## *FEAR OF GOD*

*Acts 2:43 Then fear came upon every soul, and many wonders and signs were done through the apostles.*

The fear of God will be evident. People will continually be in tears, on their face, trembling and crying out in repentance night and day. This is one reason why the prayer rooms will be full 24/7. Nobody will simply wake up, smell the coffee and proceed through another day. Yes, joy and freedom and exuberant life will be exploding out of us, but so will the severe weight of God's judgement.

The continual invitation of God's judgement will sound in our cities. We will trust Him like never before, and we will trust our own hearts less than ever before. We will cry out for God to ensure wrong things are made right. We will lay our lives in His hands and crave for the light of the Holy Spirit to invade every dark part of our lives, our churches and our cities.

Such an approach to God can't be casual. Again, it can be bold and wonderful, but we can't confront Him lightly ever again.

> *Hebrews 12:25-29 See that you do not refuse Him who speaks. For if they did not escape who refused Him who spoke on earth, much more shall we not escape if we turn away from Him who speaks from heaven, whose voice then shook the earth; but now He has promised, saying, "Yet once more I shake not only the earth, but also heaven." Now this, "Yet once more," indicates the removal of those things that are being shaken, as of things that are made, that the things which cannot be shaken may remain. Therefore, since we are receiving a kingdom which cannot be shaken, let us have grace, by which we may serve God acceptably with reverence and godly fear. For our God is a consuming fire.*

If we have effectively seen the city church developed to this point, we will be very familiar with God's fire. This consuming and scalding heat will scorch us in terrible and wonderful ways. God's purging will ruin our flesh and cause our spirits to dance!

We will find ourselves and the people in our church on our faces in great fear, humility and brokenness continually.

Repentance is such a precious gift. The closer we get to God, the more hours we are in the prayer room and the more His presence descends upon us, the more a cry of repentance resounds out of us.

The Bible talks about *groanings that can't be uttered*. This will be a supernatural expression as we encounter the severity and majesty of God.

> *Hebrews 5:7-8 who, in the days of His flesh, when He had offered up prayers and supplications, with vehement cries and tears to Him who was able to save Him from death, and was heard because of His godly fear, though He was a Son, yet He learned obedience by the things which He suffered.*

Jesus modeled an expressive and all consuming prayer life. *Vehement cries and tears* were offered to his Father. These days we don't hear such emotion in our churches as much as we should. When this type of atmosphere rules Sunday, many people may not come, or maybe they will, but one thing is certain—the job will get done.

## EVALUATION

Would you consider the atmosphere in your church to be supernaturally charged? Are people arriving hours early to lay at the altar and cry out to God? Is holiness taking precedence like never before? Are people experiencing dreams of God's judgement? Such things will certainly happen if you are appropriately on course. Again, the next element will further prove that you are or are not.

# ELEMENT EIGHTEEN
## *SIGNS & WONDERS*

*Acts 2:43 Then fear came upon every soul, and many wonders and signs were done through the apostles.*

I often hear people ask why we don't experience signs and wonders to a greater degree here in the United States. After reading this book, I believe the answer becomes much more clear. On a national level, we are still in the very early parts of Acts chapter two. We haven't arrived to the *signs and wonders* part yet.

It's when we are praying 24/7, unified, together continually, filled with the Holy Spirit, experiencing the manifestation of the presence of God and all of the other important elements of a city church, we will then experience a regular flow of signs and wonders.

Signs and wonders are primarily for the lost—to prove to them that this crazy lifestyle depicted in this book is the way to go! Being with God continually with other zealots is the plan of the ages!

*John 2:11 This beginning of signs Jesus did in Cana of Galilee, and manifested His glory; and His disciples believed in Him.*

As they see that such a lifestyle of passion results in the invasion of God in a region, many will jump at the chance to know this amazing God.

But, as we see in our current society, few people are interested in just another Sunday morning religious experience. People aren't looking for something worth living for, they are looking for a legitimate cause worth dying for!

As the power of God explodes out of a people who have paid the price of extreme participation in a missional society, others will have no choice but to look and crave!

## EVALUATION

If you have successfully made it to this stage, well done. Keep in mind that many ministries experience testimonies of healings and other miracles. This is certainly good and is a testament to God's grace. But, the question here is: Is the news media reporting on these signs and wonders? Are they powerful and continual? Is the city taking notice? If so, we're almost there!

# ELEMENT NINETEEN
## *ALL THINGS IN COMMON*

*Acts 2:44 Now all who believed were together, and had all things in common,*

The current normal church experience here in the United States is quite the opposite of having all things in common. The reason? We usually go into the church looking to get something out of it. However, when we truly grasp the greater vision of the city church, we'll truly forsake all to ensure the dream is realized.

Since it's very important for every soldier in this army to be in position, we'll take note of others who need assistance. We need them to be healthy, full of life and in position to get their job done, so we'll corporately ensure they are able to do so.

I'm not talking about mercy ministries here, but rather about a group of maturing men and women of God who aren't at all focused on paying the next bill or finding a way to survive another day. These are people who are aggressive, full of faith and fire and who won't let anything stand in the way of their participation.

As we see people like this emerging in our ministries, we'll experience a camaraderie unlike anything ever experienced before.

> *1 Corinthians 1:10 Now I plead with you, brethren, by the name of our Lord Jesus Christ, that you all speak the same thing, and that there be no divisions among you, but that you be perfectly joined together in the same mind and in the same judgment.*

Really, it's all about unity and likemindedness. As we keep moving in the same direction together, we'll learn to value each other. This value will result in a continual investment in one another.

## EVALUATION

Sit back and check out the environment. Do you see a disciplined and tightly connected army working together? Are people intent on ensuring the vision is fulfilled no matter what? Have people truly found victory over the cares of life? Is the primary fire pumping through their veins connected to the city church? If so, let's see how this amazing structure will continue.

# ELEMENT TWENTY
## *DAILY CORPORATE PARTICIPATION*

*Acts 2:46 So continuing daily with one accord in the temple, and breaking bread from house to house, they ate their food with gladness and simplicity of heart,*

The way it started is the way it continues. It's been prophesied quite a bit recently by reputable men and women of God that it will be normal for Believers to be in the church nearly every day of the week.

Many churches have closed their doors throughout the week—but this is coming to an end. It's appropriate to expect people to be in the church, the house of prayer, literally every day. As their primary responsibility they will simply crave to be there.

Additionally, we'll all be in small groups, in teaching centers and ministering in a variety of ways night and day. Truly, the 24/7 church is emerging at this very moment.

When we start to see families together with the church most every day and night of the week we'll know we're experiencing a reformation. The American demands that we have given in to will be confronted directly. No longer will we play to the calendar, but will instead see established a night and day ministry that enjoys full participation. Personal and corporate calendars will be subjected to the demands of the growing church.

One day, we'll discover that being together with our families and other fire-breathing Christians every day is much better than going to the movies, ball games, watching TV or a taking a nap on the couch. God, bring a reformation to this nation—deliver to us an ancient and emerging church experience! Launch us into Acts chapter two again!

## EVALUATION

Do you see a vital and active ministry before your eyes? Do you see people coming and going night and day? Is it a well oiled machine? Is their excitement in your region about what is going on? Are you maintaining each element, refusing to compromise any of them? Is everybody still filled? Is God's presence still thick? How are the signs and wonders going? What's the ratio of prayer hours per week per person? Come up with a workable grading system based on Acts chapter two. As we continue in this model, and refuse to slack off, we will certainly experience a shaking that will be felt around the world.

# C O N C L U S I O N

There is much more to be said on this topic. For example, I believe we will finally see churches merging, leaders surrendering their flocks to more gifted leaders while they take on a more suitable role, and the development of the five-fold ministry.

Pastors will get to pastor. A pastor may have little gifting in public speaking or teaching, but boy can they nurture people!

Teachers will be free to write and impart revelation publicly to hungry people.

On one end of town thousands of people will be at the house of prayer interceding for the nations. At the same time in another part of town others will be attending a training session. Still others will be in youth meetings, ministering to the poor, enjoying small groups and worshiping in parks.

We'll have city-wide staff meetings led by apostolic leaders. We'll all be on the same page appropriately submitted to each other and to those whom God has placed over us.

One goal, one leadership team, one church body and one huge revival!

Yes, it will take a shaking and a reformation, but I contend that we do everything we can to help give God this dream of a unified church based on His Book. Our cities and our planet will never be the same again.

# CONTACT INFORMATION

## John Burton

www.johnburton.net
john@johnburton.net

Made in the USA
San Bernardino, CA
04 August 2016